FREE TO BE

C000319768

FREE TO BE

Discovering the God of Freedom

ANDREW WINGATE

DARTON·LONGMAN + TODD

First published in 2002 by
Darton, Longman and Todd Ltd
1 Spencer Court
140-142 Wandsworth High Street
London SW18 4JJ

ISBN 0–232–52394–0

A catalogue record for this book is available
from the British Library.

Designed by Sandie Boccacci
Phototypeset in 10.25/12.5pt Times
by Intype London Ltd
Printed and bound in Great Britain by
Page Bros, Norwich, Norfolk

Contents

Foreword

This book is a testimony to what can emerge through friendship and trust within the differences of history, culture and faith. It is not only for those who are already committed to inter-faith relations but also for those who want to live a more inclusive journey at such a time as this.

I am not alone in asking, 'Who are the leaders in local government and in the faith communities with a long-term vision for our cities? How can we offer encouragement and support to those who work with what I choose to call mosaic; the mosaic with every colour distinct, vibrant and essential to the whole? Who works with discernment and courage within the frightening shadows that belong to such diversity? How are we to interpret these issues within the various sub-cultures of our cities? And what of the churches?' In Birmingham, the city where I live, a few weeks after the terrorist attacks on New York and Washington, the Inter-Faith Council issued an open invitation to members of the different faith communities: 'Bring what is now happening among your people and also bring what your religious tradition can offer to enable us to live through such a time as this.' It was a remarkable gathering. A young Buddhist presided over a complex and heated occasion where Muslim, Hindu, Jewish, Bahai and Christian leaders made their short presentations. This process of dialogue may become the sign of hope. In his book *Exclusion and Embrace*, Miroslav Volf writes from his experience in Croatia during the war in the former Yugoslavia and affirms, 'Each needs all to be itself' and 'You are not only you – others belong to you.'

Andrew Wingate is a priest, well rooted in the Anglican tradition, who is learning what it can mean to live within the freedom of the radical openness of the Gospel. The author is a great storyteller. He draws not only on encounters made during many years of travel within the communities of the world but also from what he has seen, heard and learned through living and working in Tamilnadu in South Africa, in Birmingham and now in Leicester. He is a teacher who not only helps us to see and hear the Bible stories in context and with a fresh perspective but who also brings theological insight and rigour into the urgency of our times.

When some years ago I read Andrew's retreat addresses given in Northumbria, I sensed that here was something unusual, refreshing and accessible for many people, including those not connected to the organised church. On reading the early drafts of this book I have become both convinced and even more excited. *Free to Be* is the book that many have waited for. It will challenge, encourage and inform. It is for personal reading and also for group study and meditation. It is a book to keep and also to share.

DONALD EADIE
Chair of Birmingham Methodist District, 1987–96, and
Chair of Methodist World Church Committee

Introduction

A catalyst for this series of meditations was a retreat I led at Shepherd's Dean, in Northumbria, for ordinands of Cranmer Hall, Durham. They were a very varied group of people in terms of experience, age, theological understanding and church positions. Their response to my reflections on freedom and the Christian life motivated me to work further on this theme, and this book is the outcome.

The chapters address the challenge of freedom in six aspects of life. This is not a philosophical treatise on the reality or otherwise of freedom, but a reflection on freedom as it impacts on us today. These thoughts are set within a biblical and theological framework, but the emphasis is on the personal, and how a full discovery of the gift of freedom can enrich our Christian journey. Four chapters are of this personal nature – on the themes of freedom to be ourselves, freedom to receive from others, freedom and responsibility, and freedom to allow others to be themselves. The other two chapters are reflections on two aspects of religious experience, freedom in worship and prayer, and freedom and conversion. Throughout the book, the personal is seen within community, and this interaction has been part of Christian tradition from its origins.

Each of the chapters can stand on its own, and be used for meditation in either an individual or a group setting. Six chapters would fit with the six weeks of Lent. The material at the end of each falls into two parts. The first consists of questions to encourage the reader to make the content of the chapter their own, and to use it to reflect on their own life and context. This could equally well be done alone, with another person, or in a group. The extracts that follow are from two writers who have meant a lot to me over the years. Both experienced a new sense of freedom when they found themselves outwardly more and more constrained. For Dietrich Bonhoeffer this was through imprisonment, and for Henri Nouwen through voluntary identification with the highly disabled when he joined the l'Arche Community. I hope these passages will help others as they have helped me. *Free to Be* does not end with a neat conclusion. This does not seem appropriate in a book on this theme. It ends with a quotation pointing to the future.

The content of the chapters reveals something of my experience over the last 25 years, in India, Birmingham, and now Leicester. Transforming was my work in South India, with an unusual mixture of theological teaching and prison ministry in Madurai, Tamilnadu, a city 90 per cent Hindu. Interaction has continued with the South Asian community in Britain, and this has become all the sharper after our move to Leicester two years ago. After Durban, South Africa, Leicester has the largest Hindu community outside India, and with a growing Muslim minority. Our home is in an area with about 75 per cent Muslims, mostly of Indian origin.

These experiences have made me understand that I can no longer hold my Christian faith in isolation from the religions and people around me. Christians need to grow in confidence to relate in a positive way, from friendship and not fear. This has always been the case, but many more people are understanding the necessity for such engagement since the disturbance in British cities in the summer of 2001, the events of 11 September 2001 in the United States, and the consequent 'war on terrorism'. This traumatic period has also emphasised that globalisation does not just affect economics, but every aspect of our existence, including the religious. My experience working at Selly Oak as Principal of the United College of the Ascension, a college that brings together Christians from all over the world, and my wide travels in that role, are also part of what I bring to this book.

Since my return from India my task has included encouraging Christians in Britain to break out of a religious ghetto, to learn about and understand the faiths of others, and to be confident enough to share what is distinctive in their own faith. In this book I am not suggesting that everything said about freedom is unique to the Christian Gospel, but I do believe it is at the very centre of that Gospel. My ecumenical experience, locally and globally, convinces me of that. These reflections are, I hope, rooted in theological and biblical traditions. My aim is to make them accessible to the committed, who, I trust, will be led to reflect more deeply on the challenges of freedom. I hope also that those who find themselves on the edge of church communities, and also those who are unconnected with any church but who are exploring faith, may find helpful things that address them in the confusion of life and the struggle to believe. The book may suggest open and inclusive possibilities to those who have felt alienated by a narrow exclusiveness that has become increasingly prevalent in most religions in recent years. This is what encourages many to say, if this is religion, we want none of it.

I would like to acknowledge here those who have contributed much to the experiences recorded here. I name specifically staff and students of the Tamilnadu Theological Seminary, and its principal Dr Sam Amirtham, who pushed open many doors to learning and experience for me. I mention also the prisoners of the Central Jail, who feature several times in these pages, and whose openness and friendship enabled me to cross seemingly enormous barriers of culture and faith. I acknowledge too colleagues at the West Midlands Course, Queen's College, where I was Principal for eight years, and at the United College of the Ascension, where I was for ten years. These were exhilarating places, and the varied lives of our mature students exposed me to all kinds of new contexts, in Britain and in other parts of the world.

I thank Donald Eadie for writing the Foreword. A Methodist minister in multi-cultural areas, theological teacher, former Chair of the Birmingham District, and empathetic listener and wise counsellor, Donald has supported many people on their journeys towards a freedom to be.

I mention with thankfulness the members of my family. My daughter Joanna gave me permission to write about her story, and my second daughter Jenny has been a constant critical friend. I thank my 24-year-old son Matthew, with whom I have shared the text in detail, and who offered very reflective comments. I hope his support indicates that some young people might find these chapters helpful in holding to an openness of faith, where the 'liberal' is not seen as a negative word. I thank also my wife Angela who has shared the journeys recorded in this book with me, and the moves and upheavals they represent. This includes the move to Leicester, a new city and a new type of work, which I at first found difficult. She kept me at the project when I felt able to return to writing, and saw it through to the end.

Finally my thanks are due to DLT, and its editor Brendan Walsh. In the delays in writing consequent on my move, he always understood, and made me continue to believe this was worth finishing, because of his enthusiasm about what he was reading.

Chapter 1

FREEDOM TO BE OURSELVES

Galatians 5:1–6; John 8:31–6

> For freedom Christ has set us free. Stand firm, therefore, and do not submit again to a yoke of slavery.
>
> *Galatians 5:1*

> If you continue in my word, you are truly my disciples; and you will know the truth, and the truth will make you free.
>
> *John 8:31–2*

To consider the concept of Christian freedom, and issues related to it, is a deeply evangelistic task, in the broad sense of that word. It is about the good news at the centre of the Christian life at its best. It is about the individual person, but also about the person within community, nation and the wider world. It is about the 'glorious liberty of the children of God'. It is about freedom, in the end, of the whole creation, as pointed to in the Epistle to the Romans, chapter 8, where the whole creation is seen as 'groaning as if in pangs of childbirth', as it waits in eager anticipation to be freed from the shackles of mortality. In the Epistle to the Ephesians, with its cosmic dimensions, everything in heaven and earth is to be brought into unity in Christ (1:10), and in the Book of Revelation there is the vivid picture of a new heaven and a new earth.

Yet so often the impression given is the opposite. To be a follower of Jesus Christ, or at least to be a member of the Church we call his Body, is to enter an oppressive society, concerned with preserving the past and not always the best of the past. 'As it was in the beginning, is now and always will be.' The popular view is that it is a society dominated by restrictions and negatives, to be a member of which encourages inhibition and narrowness. It is a weary kind of place. This is surely the verdict of most young people, as they pass all churches by on the other side, if they are part of a minority that has any concept of what a church is at all. Their role models lie in such areas as entertainment or sport or amongst their peer group. They know much of David Beckham or Geri Halliwell, little of Jesus Christ, and nothing of St Paul. Nor is it much different with the older generation. This is revealed especially at the occasional offices, baptism, marriage or funerals. Groups may then come to church, but their unease or complete disorientation as they come into an alien world, only reveals the enormous gap between the context of the church and the context of the world. Far from feeling free, in touch with an experience that is liberating and life-enhancing, they feel a kind of dis-ease and strangeness that merely prevents them being themselves.

I felt that recently, as an Anglican on holiday, when attending a Roman Catholic Mass in the Outer Hebrides. The atmosphere was designed to exclude the outsider, and the sermon only added to this, as it was pervaded with an emphasis on sin and concluded with the demand of Mass obligation. The moment of communion only added to the unsettled feeling. Should I take or not? Does the rule apply that it is permitted if there is no Anglican church within, is it forty or fifty miles? At the end, all rushed away, seemingly oblivious to whether I had been there or not. This is not a denominational story, and this, with variations, could have been any kind of church, and not just in the Hebrides.

Yet in John's gospel we read, 'I came that they might have life, and have it abundantly' (John 10:10), and in St Paul, 'For freedom Christ has set us free'. What is this abundant life, this freedom, that is talked about? This is the theme of the chapters that follow, the pearl of great price waiting to be discovered.

I have seen two films in recent years which challenge us to

think what it means to take hold of the gift of freedom to be ourselves. The first is *Babette's Feast*, and it is set on what appears as a rather gloomy island which is part of Denmark. The island exudes the kind of subdued pastel colours found in paintings from Scandinavia. The colours are grey, and so is life. Church and community are closely integrated, and both are as grey as the scenery. The Protestant community does not believe life is there to enjoy, but to endure. Restrictions ring-fence the community, with no excesses of any kind allowed – no dancing, drinking, feasting, laughing, courting. Food is without seasoning and wholesome, houses bare and functional. The church mirrors such a way of life, with worship that is dull, music that is a dirge, prayers about how wretched human beings are, particularly those from that island, and preaching that is condemnatory.

Into the middle of such a scene comes a mysterious stranger named Babette, a woman rumoured to come from Paris. Her problem is that she does not understand the world she has entered, because she is young and joyful, fun-loving and hopeful. But for a long time she has no choice but to conform; the context absorbs her, and she loses her sense of who she is, the freedom to be herself. She is in straitened circumstances, and has to get a job as a community cook, something she clearly knows something about. But cooking materials available are very limited and bland. Any attempt at originality is frowned upon. She can do nothing but become grey herself. She notices all the backbiting and mutual suspicion, lack of trust and friendship amongst those to whom she serves food. But she can do nothing about it except lose herself in adjusting. She thereby becomes sadder and sadder, the life goes out of her, even though no one is actually cruel to her. Life goes on drearily from day to day.

One day a letter arrives for her from Paris. She has won the lottery! Someone had been buying a ticket for her each week, and her number has come up. What is she to do? Go away, back to Paris, out of the gloom, to find herself again? No, she decides on the opposite, to try to rediscover her freedom where she is. She considers what she can offer to those with whom she lives now that she has the means. The answer is a great feast, for it is revealed that she was a cook in a famous restaurant in Paris, and cooking is her skill. Money need now be no object. She imports from France everything she needs – exotic ingredients, wines, spices, herbs and assistant cooks. At first community members object strongly. But gradually she wins them round by her infectious enthusiasm, as she increasingly rediscovers herself and becomes a magnetic personality again. One by one the bolder ones begin to join in the preparation, and even those who do not, agree with hesitation to come to the feast.

In the end it becomes a village celebration of abundant life. The food is superb, the wine is excellent and has of course a strong effect on those who had disdained even to taste a drop of wine before. More than that, in the process of preparing the feast, people begin talking to each other as they have not done for years. People forgive and are forgiven of long-festering injuries. Everything loosens and people become free. Their personalities begin to emerge in all their fullness.

Babette is happy and content, and we see her on the morning after the feast exhausted but fulfilled. She has at last offered the village the talent she has, and brought happiness to many. She has 'squandered' her money in an observer's eyes. But at another level, she has lost her life, only to find it. Her new friends ask her now what she will do with her money, and when she will be leaving for Paris. She smiles and says she will not be going to France – she has no money, it has all gone on the preparations and delivery of the feast. All she wishes to do is to remain their cook. But it is to be cook in a transformed community. People are now able to be themselves. Each can now be an individual, not conforming to an oppressive norm, but transfigured into what God created them to be. She herself has found her freedom again, not by escape into another world, but where God has now placed her in life, she has 'lost her life to find it'.

A similar message comes from a second and very popular film, *Chocolat*. This is a kind of parable set in a French village. The village is beautiful, but its beauty is blighted by the power of the mayor and his pawn the priest, who insist on imposing an oppressive morality, accompanied by strict attendance at Mass, in order to keep all power in their hands. Emphasis is on sin and its discovery, and all kinds of suspicions and quarrels become excessive, along with backbiting and disharmony. No one trusts anyone else. Into this situation comes a stranger, a beautiful Spanish woman, with a young daughter and no husband. She does not attend Mass, where indeed she would not anyway be welcome, for obvious reasons.

She opens the most exquisite chocolate shop, where she sells, but more often gives away, all kinds of chocolates which she makes herself. She also opens a café in her shop, where people drink exotic chocolate drinks and begin to talk to each other. Through her generosity, gradually feelings are brought to the surface, and deep-seated quarrels are reconciled. Eventually, through an accident, even the mayor and the priest find themselves eating the forbidden luxury and becoming more at ease. The film ends on Easter morning, when the priest casts away the doom-laden sermon he was to preach, as dictated to him by the mayor, about how the Lord would rise and smile only upon those who repented of their sins. Rather, he says more hesitantly, but for the first time speaking freely as himself, the Lord is inclusive, and on the cross and in his rising, he reveals his love for all. The film is a parable about grace, how generosity enables people to be free to be themselves and truly to begin again, and that is what we are called to be and to receive. A challenge is to reflect on our church in relationship to this parable: where are we?

Vianne, the heroine of *Chocolat*, unlike Babette, moves on to another place, a bit like Jesus in his ministry or in his resurrection appearances. The instinct is to ask her to stay, but it is now up to the villagers to carry on in the same spirit that they have been inspired by. I am reminded of John's gospel, where Jesus says that it is expedient that he goes away, that another comforter may come; or the resurrection appearances, where Jesus is always moving on. These experiences are fleeting, but life-creating. The disciples can only become themselves when they are left to follow through the implications of what they have seen, to go and tell others, to go forward to Galilee, the place of the nations.

One of the common themes in these two films is that they are about the release of feelings and emotions which have been ossified or suppressed for years. One of the striking aspects of the resurrection appearances is that they result in the release of a whole range of feelings – of awe and fear, of joy and wonder, of excitement and confusion, of certainty and doubt. We see all these in the films, as gradually people come to be themselves. As they are transformed, whether villagers or disciples, what is transformed is the whole of the person; that is what is born again.

So often religions emphasise only one part of the person. This may be 'the soul', whatever that is, that which is intangible and beyond the body, that which is seen as capable of receiving eternity. It may be 'the mind', the rational self so beloved in Western scientific and logical culture. It may be 'the body', seen as the centre of sin and selfishness, and of sexuality, with all the potential for sin there. It may be 'the will', that which determines the direction in which we will go, and again so suspect, as it so often chooses wrong directions. Or it may be 'the feelings', seen as unreliable and indicative of an amber if not a red light for the good religious person.

Major religions all have a tendency to centre upon the soul or the mind. This has often been so in Christianity, particularly in the West from the time of Augustine onwards, which has seen the body as generally sinful, and the mind as the place where God can be encountered, and the soul where eternity can be realised. The same has been the case with classical Hinduism (known as *advaita*), where *moksha* or *mukti*, somewhat akin to 'salvation', is achieved when the body is put behind oneself. We become detached from the consequences of our emotions and feelings, and reach a point of acceptance, when we realise that the ultimate and our *atman* or 'soul' are one. Then we have reached salvation. The 'realised soul' like this, when a person dies, 'leaves the body'.

Someone who not only reflected deeply in this area, but understood this philosophy from personal experience was Father

Bede Griffiths. He died in 1996, and was the *guru* of Shantivanam, an ashram in Tamilnadu, where I, as many from East and West, got to know him as a wise friend and teacher. He was an Oxford-educated British Roman Catholic priest who spent most of his ministry in India. He moved further and further in the direction of a synthesis between Eastern and Western thought, as he ventured far into classical Hinduism, as well as enabling inspirational indigenous worship in this peaceful community. A pupil of C. S. Lewis, he was a person of deep feeling, and a romantic by nature, who had sought for paradise in rural Gloucestershire with his university friends before his conversion to Catholicism. But for much of his life he felt that he had suppressed the feeling side of his personality, and even in Shantivanam he appeared to enjoy most rational discussion, a search for a Christian *advaita*, and practice of yoga-style meditation.

At the age of eighty-four, he had a major stroke. He survived this and lived for three more years, during which he felt that he learned more than in his previous 80 years. The stroke had hit the left side of his brain, his rational and logical side, with a great blow that he described as like being hit by a sledge-hammer. The result had been at first shattering. But as he recovered he made a new discovery about himself, that he had a strongly 'feminine' side, the place of emotions and feelings, and that he did not need to be afraid of this any more. This brought him closer to others, as he met them not mind to mind, but feeling to feeling. A close friend said that before his stroke, Bede was to her an ideal; after it he became real, a human being, a personal friend, one whose British reserve had at last broken down.

At the same time, through the stroke, he felt much closer to God. He discovered God as beyond male and female in essence, but as male and female in presence. This has always been the case in Hindu *bhakti* (devotional) spirituality, where both male and female aspects of the deity are worshipped in a temple. Now Bede discovered this for himself. Or rather his illness became the way of God's grace bringing this home to him. He talked of an experience of 'surrendering to the Mother', and of being 'overwhelmed by love', and how this helped him to love others as never before. He had experienced 'unconditional love' which he had often spoken of rationally before, but now knew as 'utterly mysterious and beyond words'.

In a letter written on 15 April 1990, he reflected how the stroke had been an experience in three dimensions, and this is how he now saw everything:[1]

> On the physical level it was apparently a stroke, a bursting of a blood vessel due to a lack of oxygen in the brain. On the psychological level it was a 'death of the mind' – a breakdown of the left-brain rational mind and an awakening of the feminine intuitive mind. But on the spiritual level it certainly left an impression of *advaita* – a transcendence of all limitations and an awakening to the non-dual reality. This has left an indelible impression on me. I am seeing everything in a new light.

He issued a challenge to those who are to follow him, that we should allow a balance between male and female, between the rational and the intuitive, as we live within ourselves, and within our community. The challenge is to discover the whole of ourselves without the help of a Babette, or a chocolate-maker, who may well not come to our home or community, and without the experience of having such a trauma as Father Bede suffered.

Today we seem to hear little of transactional analysis, developed by Dr Eric Berne, as a psychological tool to analyse what he calls 'ego states'. This used to be as fashionable as the Myers-Briggs tool for analysing personality is today. One aspect of such analysis is to consider how far any particular personality is a balance between 'parent', 'adult' and 'child'. The parent is the authority figure, whether nurturing or critical. The adult is the rational self, working like a computer to make objective decisions. The child is the feeling and playful one, who may be 'free' or 'adaptive'. The free child is spontaneous, fun-loving and creative, the adaptive child is rebellious or compliant and repressed, depending on how the person handles that side of personality. Each of us may vary in the degree to which we are one or the other. But all of us need all parts to be a whole person, all are essential for survival. Where our child is repressed, our feelings are repressed, and we can end by never being ourselves, and this can lead to serious consequences. Where our child is weak, we may need to let ourselves go a bit, to become the free person who is more attractive than we have allowed ourselves to become until now, to become spontaneous and joyful. If our child is excessive, we become out of balance, possibly dangerous to others and ourselves, and need appropriate control from our adult side, lest we need control from the police.

Television can reveal much, as it homes in on the external signs of how a person is. David Duval, an American golfer, won the British Open Championship in 2001. He had never won a major championship before. He was known through television as a man who never showed emotion, never smiled. He even wore shades over the front and side of his eyes, seemingly lest any glint could be seen in his gaze. There was something unnatural in all this. How much easier it was to cope with the drama of the ups and downs of another golfer who had never won a major, the Scottish golfer Colin Montgomerie, whom we felt we knew. How much more empathetic to feel the pulse of Tiger Woods, as he repeatedly punches the air with joy. What a relief therefore, when he had won the championship, to see David Duval raise his shades, brush back his hair, and break into a shy smile, as he looked across at 'his special lady' as the TV commentator put it, standing in the crowd. The man is truly human!

The call is to be what we are, where we are, not to be what we cannot be or do what we cannot do. An Afro-American writer put it, 'I try to keep telling them that the most wonderful thing in the world is to be who you are.'[2] In Christian theological terms, it is 'to grow into the measure of the fullness of the stature of Christ'. As has been expressed by the novelist Anita Shreve, 'We are all unfinished portraits.'[3] The important thing is that we feel free enough to grow, not simply in any direction, but where God challenges us to go. It may be that that challenge comes through events, through other people, through the context in which we are placed, or it may come through reflection and prayer. This will be a journey with perhaps high and low points from time to time, and often we can only see where we have come to, by looking back to where we have come from. It is never a finished journey, on this side of eternity at least. I recollect the prayer of Sam Amirtham, the Principal of the Tamil-nadu Theological Seminary, reflecting about the college: 'Lord, we are not what we ought to be, we are not what we could be, but thank you Lord, we are not what we were.'

This can be prayed by all of us in our life's journey. We will never know the end, only that we have grasped the freedom available to us where we are, to move ourselves on and have a little influence where we are. Archbishop Oscar Romero, the best-known of the many martyrs of El Salvador, wrote shortly before he died:

> We accomplish in our lifetime only a tiny fraction of the magnificent enterprise that is God's work. Nothing we do is complete, which is another way of saying that the Kingdom is always beyond us. No statement says all that could be said. No prayer fully expresses our faith. No confession brings perfection, no pastoral visit brings wholeness. No programme accomplishes the Church's mission. No set of goals and objectives includes everything. This is what we are about. We plant the seeds that one day will grow. We lay foundations that will need further development.
>
> We cannot do everything, and there is a sense of liberation in realising that. This enables us to do something, and to do it very well. It may be incomplete, but it is a beginning, a step along the way, an opportunity for the Lord's grace to enter and do the rest. We may never see the end results, but that is the difference between a master builder and the worker. We are workers not master builders, ministers not messiahs. We are prophets of a future not our own.

Such an attitude enabled Romero to feel free to live for the day ahead and trust the rest to God, to stand by the 'little ones' of his tragic country, and not to turn his back on an assassination which came when he expected, though perhaps not where he expected, as he celebrated Mass for his people. He felt free because he knew he could not control everything. How many of us are enchained because we think we can!

One of the ways we can appreciate that gift of the freedom to be ourselves is by hearing of the situation of someone who has lost that, and longs for it. Asylum seekers in Britain who have clearly come because of the lack of freedom in their own country either politically or religiously are often such people, and bring into sharp focus what we read of in the newspapers as international problems or civil strife a long way away. In Leicester an ecumenical group makes regular visits to a large hotel which is the home to many people who suffer deep trauma as a result of what they or their families have suffered for their vision of freedom for their country and their family, or their right to choose their religion. Freedom to be themselves is dependent on the context in which they are living and bringing up their family. They personify, at the time of writing, the struggles in places such as Iran, Iraq, Afghanistan, Kosovo, Somalia and Zimbabwe. Who knows which places will be represented by the time this book is published, so much pressure is there on human freedom? Kandahar, in Afghanistan, ceases to be merely a place under bombardment by the USA, as the centre of the Taliban, but the home of the person I am meeting in safety in Leicester. All becomes very real, as we hear of how he was imprisoned and tortured for six months, to force him to fight for a regime he hated, until somehow his family raised the money to bribe his jailers, and get him out through Pakistan to Britain. He has left his wife under American bombardment and dare not contact her. So also with Zimbabwe, as we hear the story of a young soldier who refused orders to beat up opposition supporters, and was consequently beaten up himself. He was told he would be sent to the Congo. Instead he came here. His father has since been found killed.

Of course, the freedom to be ourselves is not an absolute freedom. We become anarchists in terms of secular law if we do not normally submit ourselves to the laws of the state in which we are living. But when does that general instruction have to be set aside, in the interests of a greater freedom? Romans 13:1–7 offers guidance in this area. But it assumes that rulers 'are not a terror to good conduct, but to bad', and that we should therefore obey them. But what about when this is reversed, when rulers threaten good behaviour and encourage evil action and terror? Desmond Tutu and other Christians addressed this passage in particular when it was used to justify non-resistance to apartheid. It is a fine judgement to be carefully considered in the various extreme situations which so much threaten people's freedom to be themselves, such as those in the countries above.

The gospels indicate that for all disciples of Jesus Christ, the freedom to be ourselves only comes paradoxically through a willingness to lose ourselves. This was the challenge the disciples could not at first face, as they were called to take up their cross and follow Jesus to Jerusalem and Calvary. Many turned back before reaching Jerusalem, and all the men at least, except possibly one, left their Lord to carry his cross alone. They had forgotten the words to them, that 'Whoever wants to save his life will lose it, but whoever loses his life for my sake and the Gospel's will save it' (Mark 8:35). The acted parable in John's gospel, the washing of the feet in chapter 13, gives the same message. We are to become like servants, and there is no one so pushed around, in such a society as Jesus lived in, as the servant or slave. Everything is done at another's behest. That may be our calling, and all of us need to look for places where we can serve. But our voluntary and free submission is to God, 'whose service is perfect freedom'.

The call may be to give ourselves up for a cause. By surrendering ourselves to a cause greater than ourselves, something that we feel is a God-given call, we may also paradoxically find a new freedom. A woman is married to a Christian minister and he carries out his ministry in faithful service. She has no particular direction in her life, until she finds herself caught up in the cause to remove nuclear weapons from Britain. For decades she has used every means to bring pressure upon the authorities, in a single-minded commitment to a cause which she believes is deeply of the Gospel. In recent times, she has focused upon the Trident submarines, based in Holy Loch in Scotland. A television programme was made about her daring attempt to interfere with a submarine by demobilising it. This involves her, now in late

middle age, in putting on a diving suit and, at night with only
one companion, swimming across the loch with tools, to attempt
the task. She fails and is arrested, and given a suspended sentence.
But she will not promise not to do this again. In the programme,
her husband comments with resignation as she spends so much
time away from home on her cause, that that is how she is. She
believes in the cause; he could not do what she is doing and so
he leaves it to her. That is where she finds her freedom.

Mother Teresa was another example of someone who, in
finding a cause and choosing to lose herself in that cause, paradoxically found herself. Her earlier career was as a schoolteacher
in a wealthy convent school, where the elite of Bengal had their
daughters educated for high positions or high marriages or both.
She remained behind the walls of the convent during the time of
trauma which India endured in the years before independence in
1947, following a vow of enclosure herself. She became head-
mistress, and at a time of extreme violence in Calcutta on 16
August 1946, when five thousand died in a great killing and
another fifteen thousand had been wounded in the area around
her school, she broke her vow to go out to seek food for her
three hundred students, although there was a general curfew. For
the first time she chose freely to risk her life to find it, but this
was not to be her moment of life calling.

This second calling came two weeks later when she was on a
train to Darjeeling. She recorded an unmistakable summons:[4] 'It
was on that train that I heard the call to give up all and follow
him into the slums – to serve him in the poorest of the poor. I
knew it was his will and I had to follow him. The message was
quite clear. I was to leave the convent and work with the poor
while living among them. It was an order. I knew where I
belonged, but I did not know how to get there.' She quotes the
words of the fourth gospel, 'You have not chosen me, but I have
chosen you.' She writes of the 'little way' of her patron St
Thérèse of the Child Jesus: 'My little way is the way of spiritual
childhood, the way of trust and absolute self-surrender.' This is
the paradox of freedom of choice in Christ, we are most free
when we most lose ourselves in him and his calling. We are most

clear when we are freely responding to his call, when, again paradoxically, we have no choice.

It was two years before she was able to leave the convent, after she had gained an 'indult of exclaustration', to break from the enclosure with permission from her superiors in her Order and in the hierarchy of the Church, 'to reach the very poorest'. This had even necessitated writing to the Pope, 'I wrote that God was calling me to give up all and to surrender myself to him in the service of the poorest of the poor in the slums,' – a letter that the wise Archbishop of Delhi never sent on! She left her home of so many years, with a cross and a rosary, wearing sandals and a poor Bengali woman's sari, and carrying five rupees. So she began the life journey that she was to make personally, out of which came her new Order, the Missionaries of Charity. She wrote to the Archbishop:

> God wants me to be a lonely nun, laden with the poverty of the cross. Today I learned a good lesson. The poverty of the poor is so hard. When I was going and going till my legs and arms were paining, I was thinking of how they have to suffer to get food and shelter. Then the comfort of my convent came to tempt me, but of my own free choice, my God and out of love for you, I desire to remain and do whatever is your holy will in my regard. Give me courage now, this moment.

As they reflect back, those who have made this kind of decision for the future often record how they were both immensely free and freed by the way they went, and at the same time ultimately constrained as they took that step. They could do no other because of something or someone infinitely greater than themselves. This they might term 'love' or 'God' or speak of in some other way. It was the kind of experience that took Abram into the Negev desert, took him from being Abram to Abraham. It took Moses from the security of Midian to the cauldron of Egypt. It took prophets like Amos and Isaiah and Jeremiah from a life of anonymity and routine, to a place of risk and confrontation in the cause of righteousness and holiness. It took Andrew and Peter, James and John from the domesticated life of Galilean fishermen to the wandering insecurity of following a guru who insisted on risking all for the nebulous concept of the Kingdom of God. It took Mary Magdalene and the other women around Jesus away from the security of their homes to a scandalous journey serving a master who insisted that he 'had nowhere to lay his head'. It took eleven disciples resigned to disappointment away from a return to the routine of their former life in order to take up the greatest challenge imaginable, to take the Gospel to all nations. This meant beginning in Jerusalem, where they had experienced the death of their Lord, and ending in Rome, through the imperial power of which that same Lord had been crucified.

In journeys of faith, there is often a questioning of identity: who am I in all this, the one I was, the one I am, or the one I will be? Did I ever really make any choice at all? And yet in freedom I have become what I was meant to be. This may be by some dramatic change of life, as mentioned above, or it may involve no such outward change, but be an inward pilgrimage no less profound for that. Kate Compston writes a meditation in these terms:[5]

> O God, who am I now? Once I was secure in familiar territory, in my sense of belonging, unquestioning of the norms of my culture, the assumptions built into my language, the values shared by my society.
>
> But now you have called me out and away from home, and I do not know where you are leading. I am empty, unsure, uncomfortable. I have only a beckoning star to follow.
>
> Journeying God, pitch your tent with mine, so that I may not be deterred by hardships, strangeness, doubt. Show me the movement I must make towards a wealth not dependent on possessions, towards a wisdom not based on books, towards a strength not bolstered by might, towards a God not confined to heaven, but scandalously earthed, poor, unrecognised . . . Help me to find myself as I walk in others' shoes.

With all that has gone before in mind, I turn to the biblical passages mentioned at the beginning of the chapter. The word 'freedom' appears surprisingly little in the New Testament, just seven times in the epistles. The adjective 'free' comes three times only in the gospels, and twenty-two times in the epistles. Of the examples in the epistles, no fewer than nine come in the six chapters of the Epistle to the Galatians, about a third of those in the whole New Testament. Hence it is not surprising that it is known as the Epistle of Freedom, and Paul as the Apostle of Freedom, though seen in a popular way often as the Apostle of Restrictions.

When Paul becomes passionate, as in this whole epistle, it is in defence of freedom. He cannot believe that, having tasted freedom, the congregations to whom he is writing can in their right minds return to bondage. He is not urging them to choose freedom. Freedom has chosen them, as it had chosen him, on the Damascus road (1:15–16). He is truly 'astonished' that they should turn away so quickly (1:6). He sees them as 'stupid' and 'bewitched' (3:1). 'You have become free as sons, and yet you want to make yourselves slaves again' (ch.4). This is all beyond his ken. Hence his bewilderment, and indeed anger. To taste life, and then put themselves back into the cul-de-sac of death! Real freedom comes from having been chosen by Christ, and in the security of that choice, moving forward in surrender to him, losing oneself for his sake. And yet they are in danger of submitting themselves again to the yoke of slavery (5:1). Hence his ringing cry, 'It is for freedom that Christ has set us free. Stand firm therefore.'

The choice has been made, or rather has come to them. Yet daily they have to reaffirm that choice in patience, faith and hope. It is that choice towards righteousness which is always before us (v.5). Its fullness will only be known in the *eschaton*, in the fullness of eternal life. To live in freedom in this way is to live the life of the Spirit. To live by faith, and to live by the Spirit and to live in freedom are one and the same thing (v.5). Living by the Spirit is living in love (v.6) and living in freedom: 2 Corinthians 3:17, 'Where the Spirit of the Lord is, there is freedom.' And remaining in such freedom, we are called to grow more to become what God wishes us to be, as we look to the Jesus Christ who has set us free:

> And because for us there is no veil over the face, we all see as in a mirror the glory of the Lord, and we are being transformed into his likeness with ever-increasing glory, through the power of the Lord who is the Spirit (2 Corinthians 3:18).

Commenting on this passage, Tom Wright puts it thus:[6]

> We can be honest and open with one another, because the Lord whom we all worship is the Spirit, and where the Spirit of the Lord is, there is freedom.
>
> For Paul's Jewish contemporaries, the word 'freedom' meant above all else, Exodus – being set free from Egypt and sent home to the promised land. Paul believes that the real Exodus has already happened in Christ. He says therefore to the Corinthians: don't be mistaken. You are already a free people, and I as an apostle share that glorious freedom with you. And this is what comes from being the people in whose hearts God has written the law by his Spirit. This is the freedom on offer for all who are in Christ, who are indwelt by the Spirit.

In Galatians, Paul sees two dangers. The one is that freedom will mean licence, and he has a horror of this (v.13). The other danger is that of relapse, back into a slavery of our own making. This makes him even angrier than the fear of licence. For it threatens the very basis of salvation which is true liberation. Security is then found in the keeping of days and months and seasons and years, in rituals and rules, and not in 'the truth will make you free' (John 8:32). The truth lives through faith in Jesus Christ and trust in his death and resurrection, which bring ultimate freedom. The problem is not the law as gift, but the law as slave. The problem is not Abraham as the man of faith and freedom of commitment, it is in claiming a false privilege as Abraham's children (Galatians 4 and 5, and John 8:31ff.).

How ready all religions are to make ultimate what is only penultimate or even peripheral! So we become slaves to a false security. It may be in buildings: we know in our heads that we are free to pray anywhere, but in practice we are constrained by our plant. It may be in forms of prayer or ritual, and so-called 'free' worship can become fossilised and as much enslaving as set rituals. It may be in keeping certain ethical rules, which become more important than the basis of ethics itself. It may be around particular doctrines, or rather the formulation of them. It may be around certain leaders and our image of them – our Apollos, or Cephas or Paul, or even Christ. Such constraints may block us off from the all-embracing love of God, who accepts whom he wills, and not according to our rules. This is particularly relevant in the area of theology of other religions, where we are often all too ready to exclude by our own rules, provided we are sure *we* are included.

What may also hold us back, preventing us from being free, is what Paul and John both call 'sin', in the two passages mentioned at the beginning of the chapter, which have striking similarities. 'Sin' disables us because it is often accompanied by 'guilt'. We are called to be free of this if we are to grow. 'Let us lay aside every weight and the sin that clings so closely, and let us run with perseverance the race that is set before us, looking to Jesus, the pioneer and perfecter of our faith' (Hebrews 12:1–2). To move forward we have to feel forgiven and accepted by God, and so accept ourselves, love ourselves, and be able to love others, which leads to freedom through faith. 'The only thing that counts is faith working through love' (Galatians 5:6).

Not being able to forgive can also be enslaving. This is indicated in the saying: 'I will bury the hatchet, but I will remember where I have buried it.' Of course, it is easy to make moral judgements from outside about people who forgive or do not forgive. There is an amazing grace in a story of forgiveness against the odds. But those who have not suffered something of deep hurt are not entitled to judge others who find it impossible to forgive. Not all can be Gordon Wilson, who could forgive the killers of his own daughter, and find release and grace in that. Most cannot be like a parish priest whose young son was killed by a drunken driver as he walked along the pavement. He asked for the minimum sentence only for the driver, saying his sense of guilt was more than enough of a punishment. His statement in court, 'I could never again say the Lord's Prayer in public, if I did not forgive', probably had more impact than all the other sermons he had preached in his life, as it became front page headline news in all the local press. This was not only an act of forgiveness to the other, but also left the priest himself free, not to forget, but to move on.

My best friend was drowned in a boating accident that we were involved in together when we were both teenagers. My father was responsible for the party. The mixture of sadness, guilt and 'if only' feelings was overwhelming. How were we to move on? It was the mother of the drowned boy who enabled us to do so. She had me to stay on holiday, she sent presents for the following Christmas. That was all, nothing more, no words, but we could all move on in freedom.

For some, bitterness destroys their lives. We should not judge them, but be sad that that is where they remain. Sadly there is often more help for the perpetrator than the victim. The parents of the murdered toddler James Bulger seem locked in such a place. A talk programme I saw recently showed a whole group of the relatives of victims. Some were filled with a bitter hatred that was frightening. When reproduced on a corporate scale, it leads to communal wars of revenge and counter-revenge, as seen in Ireland, Sri Lanka, the Balkans, Israel/Palestine and many other places.

A third group is somewhere in between, and they are people of great honesty. They long to forgive, they long to be free, their head bids them move in that direction, as they know they are hurting themselves and cannot therefore be free. But their heart has not yet caught up with their head, and may never do so. One such is Frances Lawrence, whose husband Philip, headmaster of a Catholic school, was murdered outside his London school in 1995. She wrote an article in the *Tablet* (14 July 2001), 'What does forgiveness mean?' It ends:

> As for the question of forgiveness, I am asked about this all the time. In a sense we are all to blame for these crimes. It may be that society needs victims of a crime like this to say

that they forgive, so that society can move on, and be excused. As for my own forgiveness, I just don't know any more. When a fundamental crime against humanity has been committed, I'm not sure I know what forgiveness means, it's too profound for my human understanding. Perhaps only God knows that.

In face of such a tragedy, the ringing words in John 8:36, 'So if the Son sets you free, you will be free', and Galatians 5:13, 'For you were called to freedom brothers and sisters', may also seem too profound, perplexing or unbelievable. Such is the challenge of a faith that rests on a cross, which in human terms is the most decisive denial of freedom, but holds at the same time to the ultimate freedom beyond death of the resurrection.

Readers' response

- There is a child within each of us, whatever our age. In what ways do we express that child? Do we allow the free child to play, or do we repress our feelings and appear to have little of the child within us? How far does this prevent me 'becoming as a little child' as Jesus calls me to be?

- 'We cannot do everything and there is a sense of liberation in that' (Romero). What are the one or two things that you feel God is calling you to be or do in the immediate future, as you 'hope for righteousness', as a worker rather than a master builder?

- Who have been the Babettes of your life? Give thanks for them. Can you be a Babette to anyone else? Who?

- Is there an area related to your guilt, or the guilt of another, where you struggle to feel forgiven, or to forgive another? Reflect on whether this is preventing you being free to be what God wants you to be. Pray for release for yourself, and the grace to release the other.

Passages for meditation

Henri Nouwen, *Bread for the Journey*, p.127:

> When you are interiorly free you call others to freedom, whether you know it or not. Freedom attracts wherever it appears. A free man or a free woman creates a space where others feel safe and want to dwell. Our world is so full of conditions, demands, requirements and obligations that we often wonder what is expected of us. But when we meet a truly free person, there are no expectations, only an invitation to reach into ourselves and discover there our own freedom. Where true freedom is, there is God. And where God is, there we want to be.

Bread for the Journey, p.62:

> To be able to enjoy fully the many good things the world has to offer, we must be detached from them. To be detached does not mean to be indifferent or un-interested. It means to be nonpossessive. Life is a gift to be grateful for and not a property to cling to.
>
> A nonpossessive life is a free life. But such freedom is only possible when we have a deep sense of belonging. To whom then do we belong? We belong to God, and the God to whom we belong has sent us into the world to proclaim in his Name that all of creation is created in and by love, and calls us to gratitude and joy. That is what the 'detached' life is all about. It is a life in which we are free to offer praise and thanksgiving.

Dietrich Bonhoeffer, *Life Together*, p.86:

> But it is the grace of the gospel, which is so hard for the pious to understand, that it confronts us with the truth and says: You are a sinner, a great, desperate sinner; now come, as the sinner that you are, to God who loves you. He wants you as you are; he does not want anything from you, a sacrifice, a work; he wants you alone. 'My son, give me thine heart' (Proverbs 23:26). God has come to you to save the sinner. Be glad!

Chapter 2

FREEDOM TO RECEIVE FROM OTHERS

John 4:1–30

A Samaritan woman came to draw water, and Jesus said to her, 'Give me a drink.'

The Samaritan woman said to Jesus, 'Sir, give me this water, so that I may never be thirsty, or have to keep coming here to draw water.'

John 4:7, 15

One of my favourite possessions is a painting given to me many years ago by one of my Indian students. He is deaf, and expresses himself artistically in this way. It is in bright gouache colours, and is a representation of the encounter between Jesus and the Samaritan woman beside the well of Jacob. Its distinctiveness is its Indian style. The setting is a village well, beside which stands a very green mango tree. The well in such a village is a place of meeting. Jesus is portrayed in the saffron robes of a *sannyasi* (holy mendicant), wearing the simple sandals of a wandering pilgrim and carrying a begging bowl. He clearly has nowhere to lay his head. More boldly, he is given a blue face, the colour traditionally associated with Krishna. As I think of Krishna as an *avatar* (incarnation) of the god Vishnu, I am led here to see Jesus as, in John Robinson's words, the Human Face of God. The other figure in the picture is a woman in a sari, a village woman like countless numbers who come each day to the well in India's half a million villages, all seemingly so much the same, and yet each with their own history and uniqueness. Lesslie Newbigin, bishop of two Indian dioceses, who used to visit every corner of each, once wrote, 'Each village is different.' This is a humble place but it is the village where the patriarch Jacob had quenched his thirst. I have seen many such villages and many such women. In one sense this person is a nobody. In another sense, she is unique in her beauty as made in the image of God.

The woman has her bucket and is raising water for the stranger, in itself a common gesture of kindness. But in the context of an Indian village, there is nothing common about this at all. For the stranger is a holy man, a religious teacher, someone who by definition is of a high caste background. And the woman is an outcaste, one whom Gandhi called a 'harijan', less flatteringly known as an 'untouchable', one who in today's sensitised world has taken on the name Dalit ('a crushed one', but at least so named by themselves and not by others). Village wells are places of age-long clash between communities, as they fight for scarce resources, particularly when each caste does not have its own well. As I see the well, I think of one such in a village I visited that for weeks was polluted with human excrement by high caste landlords. They were trying to force back the Dalit villagers who used that well into bonded (*de facto* slave) labour. The villagers felt their conversion to Christ should also be a liberation from slavery. The peaceful scene on the painting is one of potentially deep conflict.

Yet here, Jesus does not offer anything at first to the woman, out of pity for her status. He asks for her help. He receives from her the water his thirsty body needs. To receive from someone in such cultures is to show respect to the giver. In Asian culture it is indeed hurtful to refuse hospitality, for to reject what is given is to reject the giver. This is one reason why diabetes is called the pastors' disease in South India, so essential is it that they not only pray in each house they visit but also receive a cup of sugary tea or coffee. To refuse this is to say, you are not worthy to serve me. I remember receiving a bottle of village cola in a mud and wattle house once. When I opened it, the liquid smelt of bad eggs. I was relieved to see the floor of the house was baked mud and dust. In an unnoticed

moment, I poured it away. What I could not do was to refuse it
in the first place. For Jesus to receive this water was a re-
volutionary act, it was saying that I accept you as you are and
for what you can give me.

What barriers were crossed in this simple gesture of
receiving! Four of the most impenetrable walls known to human-
kind. There is the barrier of caste, as already mentioned: 'Jews
have no dealings with Samaritans.' The Samaritans were prod-
ucts of a racial mixing going back centuries, between the left-
behind communities and their conquerors, when pure Jews had
been in exile in Babylon. To be in association with them was
to become polluted. This was one more example of the scapegoating of a community so often seen in history. It is found
today in relation to visible communities – for example, black
people in many contexts – and to seemingly invisible communities – such as, in Japan, the Burakamin (a kind of 'untouchable'
group). It is found in relation to such vulnerable groups as the
disabled or single parents or those with AIDS. Tragically it has
been found so often in relation to Jews themselves, as history
has since unfolded. The particular horror of such scapegoating
is that a whole class of people is condemned before the individual is considered. Yet Jesus allows himself to risk pollution,
he receives water across such a barrier.

There is the barrier of religion. The Samaritans were in
practice people of another faith as far as the Jews were concerned. They had gone their own way, they accepted only the
Pentateuch, the first five books of the Bible. Their ways of
worship were different. Religions so often have divided people
deeply, particularly those who are not so far apart from each
other, as found, for example, in the Jewish/Christian and Muslim
family of 'religions of the book'. The Samaritans were not
orthodox and therefore to be avoided. A parallel is the attitude
of a group of 'born again' Christians who tell those they baptise
to avoid having fellowship with 'Hindus, Muslims, Jehovah's
Witnesses, Roman Catholics, and Liberal Christians'. Religion
here is lifting up the drawbridge between people and leaving
an uncrossable moat.

I think of the barrier of sin. The Samaritan woman had sinned much; Jesus knew this, and in the course of their discussion, brought her to face it. But he did not see this as a barrier to their encounter. It was a place to start from, not a place to end with. It was a question of what she could become, not what she had already done. She was like another woman, 'the woman of the city who was a sinner', who in Luke 7 scandalised the Pharisee hosting a dinner party for Jesus by bursting in and anointing Jesus' head, weeping tears over his feet and wiping them with her hair. We can imagine the intimacy of such gestures in the middle of this crowded and respectable room. To the horror of those around him, however, he not only defended the woman, but said that the love he had received from her was a sign of her longing for forgiveness, indeed it was the opening for her salvation. His host had pointed out the barrier he should have erected: 'If this man were a prophet, he would have known who and what sort of woman this is who is touching him, for she is a sinner.' She was a labelled person, so beware. But Jesus was willing not only to forgive her, to accept her, to give to her, but, far worse, to receive from her and in such a special way, thereby showing that there is not a certain class of 'sinners' by whom one should not be touched: 'All have sinned and fallen short of the glory of God.'

Finally there is the barrier of gender. Throughout most cultures for most of human history, women have been considered inferior to men, and this has applied as much within religions as in wider societies. Men are the givers, women the receivers. Men make the important decisions, women obey. Men lead, women follow. Men are traditionally the priests, women are faithful laity. All kinds of arguments are used to rationalise such a hierarchy, but it crosses every religion. I think of the magnificent Hindu temple in Neasden where, when I visit, any men with me can go into the special sitting room of the male priests and have dialogue with them, and this will include guests with no theological background, but the highest qualified woman will have to follow an alternative programme. It is all politely done, but the barrier is absolute. So it is in a prominent mosque in Birmingham, where the imam explains why the facilities do not allow him to have women at prayer, even in the balcony, 'lest the men be distracted'. So it is in the Christian church where rules on whether women can be ordained may vary, but in practice their inferior position appears to be endemic in every place where power comes into play. So it was in the Jewish society of Jesus' time. No wonder the disciples were taken aback that a Jewish teacher was talking with a woman. They murmured even more about this than that he was talking with a Samaritan and a sinner! Yet he not only talked with her, he received from her. As a man he was not all self-sufficient, which of course no man is, but he was actually willing to show by his actions that he admitted this!

This story has universal appeal. I was surprised on my first visit to the Jain Centre in Leicester, a splendid converted church, to be shown the beautiful stained glass windows – a magnificent adjustment to the British contextual context – illustrating the life story of the founder of Jainism, Mahavira. One of them portrays Mahavira receiving food from a dark slave girl. He had been fasting and was to break his fast only when he met a person of purity. The woman turned out to be that person. Barriers here are broken down, of caste, colour and gender. However, there is one difference from the Samaritan woman. The Jain figure is pure, this was not so with the woman of Samaria. Perhaps the barrier of moral purity was the hardest to cross.

It was the story of the Samaritan woman that became the catalyst for the conversion of the great Indian convert, Pandita Ramabai, a young Hindu woman who was open to receiving love at critical moments in her life. She went on to receive life-changing experiences through witnessing that love in action with the poor, and saw here a direct link with the biblical scriptures that she was reading. Being a woman, she is much less well known within and outside India than her more famous male counterpart Sadhu Sunder Singh, with whom she can be compared as saints of the formation of the Indian church. From a high Hindu caste and from a religious family, she found herself being brought up in a Christian household in Calcutta after the death of her parents from cholera. She learned English and, being independent minded, studied Sanskrit, an unheard

of and scandalous thing for a woman to do in the late nineteenth
century. Only the highest caste males were officially allowed to
learn this beautiful and holy language. She went to England
already sympathetic towards the Christian faith and taught in
Cheltenham Ladies College. While there she went to Fulham
and witnessed the work of Christian women in the care and
rehabilitation of what were known then as 'fallen women'.
Coming from a society where at that time such women were
totally untouchable, she received deep inspiration from such
caring love. At the same time, she imagined Jesus reaching out
across the same barriers that she could see in front of her in
Fulham. She wrote of the experience:

> I had never heard or seen anything of the kind done for this
> class of women in my own country . . . I asked the Sister to
> tell me what it was that made the Christians care for and
> reclaim the fallen women. She read the story of Christ
> meeting the Samaritan woman . . . I realised after reading
> the 4th chapter of St John, that Christ was truly the Divine
> Saviour he claimed to be, and none but he could transform
> and lift up the downtrodden womanhood of India and of
> every land.

From this receiving, she became a disciple of that same Christ
and was baptised an Anglican. But before long she felt a far less
positive message from the church, and as she returned to India
she wrote:

> No one can have any idea of what my feelings were at
> finding such a Babel of religions in Christian countries . . .
> I did not adhere to any particular sect nor do I do so now.
> It was enough for me to be called a Christian on the ground
> of my belief in Christ as the saviour of mankind.

Ramabai dedicated her life to the uplifting of women in British
India, where she did a survey and found that less than 1 per cent
could read. She founded a women's university and various projects to care for lower-class women, from whom she would
normally be separated by the barriers of caste, religion and
culture. She also became the first woman member of the Indian

Congress Party and joined the beginnings of the independence struggle. She was named Pandita ('the learned one') by her Hindu colleagues. This remarkable work had all begun because of her willingness to be transformed by sights she experienced in the slums of London.

Both Ramabai and Sadhu Sunder Singh, the great Sikh convert of the same period, found one of the saddest aspects of their conversion was that the Church to which they had converted seemed to live in a different world from the one of Jesus which they experienced in the gospels. The missionary movement, they and many like them felt, was incapable of receiving from those they encountered in other cultures, such as they found in India. They were all too ready to offer a Westernised church, but very reluctant to feel they had anything to learn from their encounter with ancient religions and cultures. This has been the experience of many of those who have received the blessings of the Church, in Asia or Africa or elsewhere. The motivation to give has been very high, while, with some notable exceptions, the ability to receive has been minimal. Some of the exceptions are found in an inspiring book by Kenneth Cracknell, *Justice, Courtesy and Love*.[1] He reflects upon how experience in Asia for a number of nineteenth-century missionaries brought conversion from an exclusivism that knows the truth and has nothing to receive, to a Christ-centred inclusivism. This meant being willing to receive from the Spirit of Christ, whom they felt strongly was there in an unacknowledged way, before their arrival, amongst the people they encountered.

This openness to receiving water from the Samaritan woman leads to a dialogue through which she receives something infinitely more important, the living water of eternal life, something Jesus alone can give. Yet through that same dialogue he also receives. He comes to the deeply radical insight about the nature of true worship that the place does not matter, whether it is held at Mount Gerizim of the Samaritans or Jerusalem of the Jews. What matters is whether the worship is 'in spirit and in truth'. At a stroke he undercuts the linking of authentic worship with particular rituals or locations, or perhaps even religions. How radical and freeing this can be, is seen when we reflect on the conflict in Ayodhya, North India, and the thousands who died in 1992 and 2002 because worship must be there, whether in a temple or a mosque. Yet we have ever since often forgotten this, as we have insisted that true worship must include whatever we believe is sound, from our particular churchmanship or bias. We will return to this theme in the following chapter, on worship and prayer. We have all erected our own barriers, in the name of the same Christ who broke them down in this encounter with the Samaritan woman. Dialogue is often an excuse to give our ideas; Jesus through dialogue was able to receive transforming insight.

New Testament examples abound of the way Jesus received from those he encountered. He receives an example of faith beyond anything in Israel from a Roman centurion, a member of an occupying force, whose servant was sick (Matthew 8:5–13). Jesus gives, but he also receives. Jesus observes a widow in the temple (Mark 12:41–4) and sees her giving two coins in offering. He receives inspiration from her as someone who gave her all. I heard a South American theologian saying that in this story he felt that Jesus did not just see an example of the Gospel in action, but that this woman was herself 'Gospel', 'good news' for those who lived in his kind of marginalised situation. Jesus finds encouragement and examples in his ministry often from those whom others would most despise. These are those whose names we do not even know – the centurion, the leper who gave thanks, the poor widow; yet the inspiration they gave lives on and points us to eternity. Jesus is free and not blocked by prejudice from seeing God in strange places. He found something to receive from these people, and that is why we read of them two millennia later.

The great sacrament of receiving is that recorded in John 13. Here Peter is told that he cannot be part of Jesus and his community unless he will receive from Jesus, unless he will allow his feet to be washed. Like so many religious people, Peter preferred to do something for another, to wash his master's feet, he did not want to be under obligation, to acknowledge his need for receiving. Some black-led churches make this act of washing the third sacrament. They do not break bread in holy communion without symbolically repeating the washing ceremony. They

claim that there are three dominical sacraments, actions com-
manded by Jesus: 'Baptise in the name of the Father, Son and
Spirit', 'Take, eat, this is my body; do this in remembrance of
me', and 'Wash one another's feet.' In some mainline churches,
feet-washing takes place on Maundy Thursday. Often it is not
easy to get volunteers to have their feet washed by the priest.
There is some of that reluctance felt by Peter.

In the heat and dust of the East, it is normally the servant's
task to wash the feet of the master as he enters the house. Here,
it is the rabbi, teacher, master who is to do the washing. Indeed,
as Peter had exclaimed at Caesarea Philippi, it is the Messiah,
the Son of God, who is to wash our feet. We are required to
receive across an extraordinary barrier here. We are not to serve
the one whom John calls the very Logos, or Word of God, we
are to be served by him, to receive from him. How hard this is,
when we have been taught that we are not worthy to gather up
the crumbs from his table. It needs a freeing, a deep liberation,
to be able to receive the healing touch of the Messiah in this
way. Only if we can do this from him can we be freed to receive
from others, to receive help, encouragement, counsel, hope.

There is a sacred space between me and the other. I can receive
from that space, if I am free enough to do so, and if I have the
eyes, ears, mind and imagination to open up that space. Or it
can become an infinite gap. The choice is mine; to take it may
bring transformation.

Here are three examples of those who took that step. Henri
Nouwen was a priest and a professor at Yale and then at Harvard.
Immensely respected in his field of pastoral theology and as a
writer, after a breakdown he left to join a l'Arche community,
a place where so-called abled and disabled live together and
receive from each other. Here, Nouwen discovered extraordinary
blessings in his friendship with Adam Arnett, a 25-year-old man
who could not speak or move without assistance and who had
frequent fits. Terrified at first of the responsibility of looking
after Adam every day, Henri gradually found a stillness and
presence in Adam that could receive all the thoughts and
struggles Henri was going through. He seemed to 'call me back
to stillness at the eye of the cyclone'. Adam became for him the

heart of God, receiving all he put upon him. When Adam died, Nouwen reflected, 'Here is the man who, more than anyone else, connected me with my inner self, my community, and my God. Here is the man I was asked to care for, but who took me into his life and into his heart in such an incredibly deep way. Here is my counsellor, my teacher, and my guide, who can never say a word to me but taught me more than any book, professor or spiritual director. Here is Adam, my friend, my beloved friend, the most vulnerable person I have ever known and at the same time the most powerful.'[2] By becoming open to receiving from the most unlikely of places, Nouwen discovered himself.

This is not unusual at l'Arche. Jean Vanier, the founder of the movement gave the Lenten message to Pope John Paul II in 2002 (as quoted in the *Tablet*, 2 March 2002), in which he said:

> We are often filled with prejudices, closed up behind protective walls or barriers. We have difficulty forgiving others when they have hurt us. We frequently want power over others who quickly become rivals. Sometimes we are angry or in depression. Antonio (a young man with severe mental and physical disabilities) showed us how to accept our limits and to work with them so that we become more whole. If you had visited Antonio he would have touched you by his smile, his self-acceptance, his thirst for love and friendship. You would also have been touched by the young volunteers alongside him. If you asked them, 'Is it difficult to be with Antonio and to care for him?', you might have been surprised by their answer. 'I had been taught to be strong, assertive, agressive, so that I could get a good job. Later, at work, I had to struggle, to be the best, in order to climb the ladder of promotion, and have more money. Antonio has led me into a completely different world: the world of community and mutual listening, of growth in compassion, where each person is important, however weak, able, or disabled.'

Another such place was in the circus, where Nouwen learned from clowns and trapeze artists. Of the clowns, he remarks:

But the clown saves us: he is our man, because he fails like
we do, he makes mistakes like we do, he says to us, non-
virtuosity is OK too. And in his white face we recognise
ourselves in our daily tasks of which so many fail. Christ
is the clown who came into our circus and made us laugh
because he came to tell us that we are not what we perform.
He came for the crying, the persecuted, the weak, the hungry,
the poor. He who is called to be a minister is called to be
a clown.[3]

And from the acrobats whom he knew, known as the Flying
Rodleighs, he learned of the need to be 'totally present to the
present'. Both the trapeze fliers, and those who receive them –
and particularly the latter – were 'a symbol of the concentrated
meditative life which offered, in the same instant, both a sense
of temporal freedom and a glimpse of eternity'. He discovered
a new way of seeing and experiencing the divine: 'I can only fly
freely when I know there is a catcher to catch me. If we are to
take risks, to be free, in the air, in life, we have to know there's
a catcher. We have to know that when we come down from it
all, we're going to be caught, we're going to be caught, we're
going to be safe. The great hero is the least visible. Trust the
catcher.'[4]

Jack Grant came from a white colonial home in Trinidad, a
good Christian family, a place where you were kind to local
blacks, where you worked for their uplift, but you were definitely
in a different and superior place to them. As he grew up, he
discovered a great gift for cricket and in time became captain of
the West Indian cricket team, in the years after World War Two
when only a white man could have that post. But in his leadership
he refused to separate himself from his mainly black team-mates.
He describes how he not only respected them as great cricketers,
but also discovered in them friends from whom he could receive
encouragement and inspiration. It was this willingness to
receive at such a formative period that changed the direction of
his life. He went to work as an educationalist in South Africa
and then in illegally independent Rhodesia. In both places, he
worked tirelessly on the side of black people as they struggled

to gain their freedom. He was eventually declared an unwelcome person in Rhodesia and became the first General Secretary of the newly established African Council of Churches. All happened because Jack had been willing not to give, but to receive across the rigid colour divide.

A third example comes from the Madurai Central Jail in Tamilnadu, South India, where I worked as a chaplain, along with my theological students. Two high-caste prisoners were convicted of murder and given life sentences. They were desperately downcast, since the crime had been fixed upon them. They were big landowners and used to employ Dalit (so called 'untouchable') labourers in an area where caste divisions were enormous. In the jail they found themselves living in one barracks with people of all castes. They did not know where to turn, in their physical, mental and spiritual lostness. It was then that a fellow prisoner offered his help. He put his arms round them, befriended them, counselled them and shared his food with them. He led them out of the depths of despair. And to their horror, they found that their benefactor was a dhobi, a washerman, someone untouchable because he was in contact with dirty clothes. But they swallowed their pride and continued to receive. Eventually they responded to his invitation to join a Christian prayer group that he convened. They knew nothing of Christianity, and even he was a Hindu. But he said they should come for the fellowship. This warmth they received, and as the months went by, they were converted to faith in a God who could enable them to forgive even those who had landed them in jail. Their appeal was eventually upheld and they left the jail as free men. When asked whether they would then take baptism, they said they would wait until they could take it publicly with their dhobi friend on his release. For they believed that baptism was baptism into a Christ in whom there is no Jew nor Greek, no slave nor free, no high caste nor untouchable. Their personal transformation began with a simple act of receiving.

In my own ministry key directions have come from receiving from the unexpected. Amongst other reasons, my calling to ordination came through receiving from two persons who would be amazed to know their significance in my life. The bishop came to the church I was worshipping in. He challenged the congregation because it had produced no ordinands for years. An elderly lady, of little education or wealth, but of deep spirituality, happened to be sitting next to me and whispered into my ear at the end of the sermon, 'What about you?' In another parish I attended, the priest was much criticised because he was shy and not a social leader. But I used to watch him and the way he led the liturgy, prayed and listened to his people. I felt like the Shunammite woman in 2 Kings 4:8ff., as she observed Elisha going back and forth on his journeys: 'There goes a man of God.' I had already received quiet inspiration from this priest, and so when he challenged me about whether I was satisfied with the direction of my life, I responded with an openness that led me eventually to prepare for ordination.

Three pivotal steps I have taken in ministry have been into adult education, to India and in the area of interfaith dialogue. None was planned, all began with unexpected receivings. My adult education career, which has continued ever since, began when I was a curate and I found a College of Further Education in my area. I wandered in one day, green and hesitant in my new dog collar. I was made to feel at home by the Welsh Vice Principal who saw me wandering like a sheep without a shepherd. He received me with warmth and we became friends. He revealed that he was an atheist, but that he wanted me to teach a course there. I queried whether anyone would want to come to a course on Christianity. He encouraged me, 'You teach it, I will get the people in.' We decided on the title 'Christianity – can it survive the twentieth century?' Over thirty people came, courses followed term by term, and when I left the atheist Vice Principal persuaded the authorities to appoint a part-time chaplain! All from an act of receiving.

My call to India came from a friend at theological college who was an Indian Roman Catholic in the process of becoming an Anglican. He used to babysit for our daughter. One day, he said to me, 'Come over and be with us in India. Share your ministry with us, and learn from us.' From this beginning came not only a friendship that meant that my son became my friend's godson, and his mine, but also the transforming experience of my life.

My call to Muslim–Christian dialogue came equally unexpectedly. I arranged for a group of my theological students at Queen's College, Birmingham, to go to a local Muslim centre for an evening of discussion about prayer in our two faiths. The speaker from the Islam side was a Scottish convert, immensely learned, who proceeded to lecture us at enormous length, scrawling Arabic words on the board that none of his listeners understood. He did not want to listen but only to pronounce. My heart sank as I became aware of the enormous communication gap and the growing resistance amongst my students to a not particularly subtle attempt to show the superiority of Islam. This dialogue group I was attempting to start was going to be the shortest-lived ever! At the end, the students left with relief. There was a gentle-looking British Pakistani man who had sat quietly through the evening. He asked me whether I would like to go to his small mosque and meet some of the children he was teaching. I said yes without much enthusiasm, and fixed a day. He lived in a very poor area of town, and it was with some trepidation that I knocked on the door of his house mosque on a grey November evening. But I was received with great warmth, and for the next six hours went on visits – from the mosque to his house, where I received a meal, and to the houses of two of his friends. I finished the evening understanding the truth that I knew in theory: the principle that dialogue begins when people meet people, and not when religion meets religion. So began the long series of meetings that led to my writing a book, *Encounter in the Spirit*,[5] and a lifelong pilgrimage in interfaith relations.

In our life and ministry, so much enrichment can come if we can learn to receive from others. The hardest place for this may often be from those closest to us. Are parents prepared to learn from their children, to receive from them? It is inbred in us perhaps, to believe that 'when I was a child, I thought as a child, but when I became an adult I put away childish things.' Then how can I learn from my children? I remember being told by my daughter, then about ten, that a particular sermon was about right. I asked why, and she said it was three minutes about God, three minutes of story, and three minutes about life. I have never forgotten this moment of receiving, and always borne it in mind. Yet one of the joys is how our children grow up, and as they do so, they become our friends, our confidants, those from whom we receive advice and support. This does not happen in any planned way. Where it happens it is a wonderful thing. When a parent is unable to receive from a child, whether still a child or an adult, one of the greatest possibilities in human relationships is blocked off.

Perhaps even more so is the case with spouses. So often things go wrong when one party thinks they have little or nothing to receive from the other, and this will very often be the man, who feels a strong male self-sufficiency and thinks that to ask for help is to show weakness. And receiving from a spouse will include not just receiving friendship and love, but being prepared to receive criticism where appropriate, to hear the truth told in love. It will mean admitting that we may actually be wrong on something.

For clergy it is often difficult to be willing to receive from lay people. The clergy are expected to be the professionals, the resource persons, the ones who give to others. It is laity who are expected to be the receivers. But it is a great liberation to be able to receive. I think of a particular elderly lady who comments on every sermon I give. She does not know how much she is offering, when so many pass by all one's efforts without a comment. I think of another lay person who used to take what was said seriously enough to discuss and argue and reflect with me. I remember at theological college being sent on hospital visiting. Each of our group of students in turn had to give a 'message' to a crowded ward on a Sunday evening, not an easy thing to do. A friend was asked to do this one evening. He gave a careful exposition about Christians and suffering. An old man in bed called me over and said, 'Please tell your colleague not to talk to us about suffering. We know more about that than he does, that is why we are here. Ask him to tell us about the love of God and his care for us, then we will listen.' I passed the message on, but I received much from this, and indeed remember what he said to me more than a quarter of a century later.

It is difficult too for a teacher to learn from a student, not just facts, but about himself or herself. In the hottest part of India, where we lived, I used to keep going each day by having a siesta after lunch, along with the rest of the seminary. This time was sacrosanct. One day I was deep in sleep at 2 p.m., when someone knocked at my door. Angry, I reluctantly opened it, as the knocking persisted. It was one of my ministerial students and he had beside him a Hindu prisoner's wife on the way to the jail to visit her husband. She fell at my feet as a mark of respect. I told her to get up and go, and spoke harshly to my student about waking me up for someone whom he could have dealt with himself. I returned to my sleep. In the evening, the student came to me and quietly said how ashamed he was of how I had behaved. He pointed out that the woman had probably never met a Christian pastor before, let alone someone known as a missionary. What would her image now be, not only of a pastor, but of the Christ he represented? In the Indian context, where this is not the kind of thing a student says to his teacher, who is like a guru, such a statement took some saying – and for me, some receiving. But I have never forgotten it, and the student became a teacher to me in my ministry.

A place where I have experienced much receiving is across cultures. But this requires a willingness to set aside a sense of superiority, the belief that my culture or my religion is self-sufficient and superior, and has no need of the other. It means being ready to receive inspiration across such barriers.

An example is a Sikh teacher I know. He gives all his spare time activity to leading worship and preaching in a local Sikh *gurdwara*. He welcomes any groups I take along to experience Sikhism. Each evening probably two hundred persons gather for prayer. He will expound the Sikh scriptures and sing *bhajans* to his congregation. When I go as a Christian priest, when the formal prayer is over, he will call me forward to speak to his congregation. I will read a passage from the New Testament, and try to link it with what he has been saying. If I have an Indian Christian student with me, I will take him forward to sing a Christian song. Afterwards, we will share a meal and then engage in a dialogue of faith. Here I am very conscious of receiving much. I receive a welcome, and I receive trust as he gives a place to me in his worship. I receive hospitality and friendship. I receive too a theological challenge. Do I bring God to this place, or is he there before my arrival as I take off my shoes to enter the prayer hall? If the latter, can I be said to pray or worship in this place of Sikh faith, and am I betraying Jesus Christ? Or is he there as the Word of God, incarnate in the hearts of those faithful Sikhs? Is the Spirit 'the go-between God' as we talk together? To be confronted with such questions as I go away is truly to have received something important.

Allowing Jesus to wash our feet is not just about receiving help and sustenance, peace and refreshment from him. It is not just about receiving a sense of renewal. It is also about being radically changed by the encounter with Jesus. To return to the story with which I began this chapter, the Samaritan woman, is it too bold to say that Jesus was changed by the dialogue with her, that this was one of the transforming moments of his ministry in two directions? Here, as we saw earlier, he came to see that true worship was not about place and ritual but about quality and truth. At the same time, he perhaps realised in a radical way how there are no boundaries to the saving love of God. This Samaritan woman was one of the vehicles of this revelation, in St John's gospel at least. Here is shown the working through of the conviction expressed in the prologue to the gospel, that 'All things came into being through him, and without him not one thing came into being' (1:3). This woman, whose name we do not even know, helped to show him this, as the Spirit became the unseen third person in their encounter. She is a Johannine equivalent of the woman in the Synoptic gospels who would not accept the limitations placed on Jesus' ministry, whether by himself or by others, that he was sent only to the lost sheep of the house of Israel (Matthew 15:21–8). He was disturbed here by a woman of another faith, this time a Canaanite rather than a Samaritan, someone even further from his own Jewish faith. It is said that Jesus marvelled at her faith. Matthew, this most Jewish of gospels, becomes increasingly open to the universality of the message of Jesus and the Kingdom of God that he in-carnated. Because of brave women like these and Jesus' recorded willingness to listen to them, the early Church felt it was following Jesus truly, when it undertook the mission task of proclaiming the Gospel to all nations. It is because of nameless persons like these, who challenged exclusive barriers to the ministry of the Church at different stages in the history of the world Church, that the majority of those who are so are Christians today.

A final picture of receiving to leave with you. The Eucharist is *the* place of receiving as we hold out our hands and recite the prayer, 'We do not presume to come to this your table, merciful Lord, trusting in our own righteousness, but in your manifold and great mercies. We are not worthy so much as to gather up the crumbs under your table, but you are the same Lord whose nature is always to have mercy.' I heard of a priest who had visited Mother Teresa's home in Calcutta. He was asked to lead the Mass, and as Mother Teresa came to receive the bread, he saw on her face the same look of rapt attention and receiving that he had seen the previous day. Then he had been asked by her to visit her special people, those 'little ones' who were closest to dying, in the ward she visited most. Here she held the dying body of an old woman, and looked with such attention and love into her face. In the poorest of the poor, as we know, she found the face of Jesus. She received the love of God there and in her daily receiving of the Eucharist. The Oxford father William Pusey wrote during the nineteenth century in similar vein, 'If we would see him in his sacraments, we must see him also wherever he has declared himself to be, and especially in his poor. In them also he is "with us" still.'

Readers' response

- In quiet, think of three persons whom you feel you have been free enough to receive from. Give thanks for them each in turn, and be quite specific about what you have received from them. It might be some quite concrete assistance, it may be something general like encouragement or hope, it may be that they have been instruments in significant changes in your life or thinking.

- Think what barriers were crossed as you received from these people. Think how you felt at the time. Are you someone who finds it difficult to receive help or to listen to others? Be honest with yourself as you reflect about this. Are you blocking off the possibility of change for yourself?

- Who is your catcher? Whom do you catch? Reflect on experiences of both.

- How far are your prayers about giving to others? Or how far are they times when you open yourself up to receiving from God and from others?

Passages for meditation

Henri Nouwen, *Bread for the Journey*, p.111:

Receiving is often harder than giving. Giving is very important: giving insight, giving hope, giving courage, giving advice, giving support, giving money, and most of all, giving ourselves. Without giving there is no brother-hood and sisterhood.

But receiving is just as important, because by receiving we reveal to the givers that they have gifts to offer. When we say, 'Thank you, you gave me hope; thank you, you gave me a reason to live; thank you, you allowed me to realise my dream,' we make givers aware of their unique and precious gifts. Sometimes it is only in the eyes of the receivers that givers discover their gifts.

Dietrich Bonhoeffer, *Life Together*, p.75:

Christians, especially ministers, so often think they must always contribute something when they are in the company of others, that this is the one service they have to render. They forget that listening can be a greater service than speaking.

He who can no longer listen to his brother will soon be no longer listening to God either; he will be doing nothing but prattle in the presence of God too. This is the beginning of the death of the spiritual life, and in the end there is nothing left but spiritual chatter and clerical condescension arrayed in pious words.

Christians have forgotten that the ministry of listening has been committed to them by him who is himself the great listener and whose work they should share.

Chapter 3

FREEDOM IN WORSHIP AND PRAYER

Exodus 19:7–25; Hebrews 12:18–24

The Lord said to Moses, ' . . . you shall set limits for the people all around, saying, "Be careful not to go up the mountain (Sinai), or to touch the edge of it." '

Exodus 19:12

You have come to Mount Zion and to the city of the living God, the heavenly Jerusalem . . . and to Jesus, the mediator of a new covenant.

Hebrews 12:22, 24

Today's Christians tend to focus on a personal and loving relationship with Jesus, and on the fellowship found in contemporary understandings of the Holy Spirit. For this reason among others, this passage from Exodus makes us feel uncomfortable, emphasising as it does very different aspects of God. It is a strange yet challenging passage for the modern reader, and draws us deep into the question of how we relate to God and how God relates to us, and the question of freedom within that relationship.

The passage describes a very early theophany, the nature of which we will examine in the next few paragraphs. A theophany is a special appearance of God, and this often takes place in the midst of a storm, in this case in cloud, thunder and lightning. The circumstances of the appearing only add to the emphasis on God as the mysterious, awesome and almighty one, to be feared rather than loved, to be obeyed rather than to be in close relationship with. It is considered to be a very early piece of writing and scholars see it as similar to descriptions found in the Ugaritic texts of the near Middle East. Ugarit was a city in north-west Syria which was destroyed around 1230 BC and early potsherds have been discovered in recent times in a place now called Ras Shamra which bear a striking likeness to early Hebrew language and scriptures such as this passage. We enter here into the mists of time, and find some very early evidence of how the Israelites experienced God.

This appearance takes place on a mountain, as often happens in religious experience. We can compare it with Moses' first experience of the Lord in the burning bush which was equally mysterious and took place on the same mountain, variously named Horeb or Sinai (Exodus 3). There Moses is given a glimpse of the nature of God, not in a visual encounter, but in God's enigmatic self-description, 'I am who I am' or 'I am what I am' or 'I will be what I will be'. Another encounter on a mountain was that of Elijah when he was sheltering in a cave, believing he alone had been faithful to the Lord, on the same Mount Horeb. In the well-known passage in 1 Kings 19, Elijah experiences the full regalia of a theophany in strong wind, earthquake and fire, but finds the Lord remarkably in 'a still small voice'. We prefer to remember perhaps the beauty of that phrase rather than the bloodthirsty character of the message that follows from that same small voice!

Three further examples of theophanies are those to Abraham in Genesis 18:1–15, Jacob in Genesis 28:10–17 and Hagar in Genesis 16:7–14. In all three the atmosphere is a gentle one. In the first, the Lord appears in the guise of three men, who bring the amazing message to Sarah that she will have a child in her old age. They are both homely guests and full of mystery as to their origin and destination, and this enigmatic character of the encounter is superbly glimpsed in the much reproduced Rublev ikon. The appearance to Jacob at Bethel happens when he is asleep as he wanders in the desert. He dreams of a staircase to heaven, with the Lord above it blessing him and assuring him of his continuing presence and commitment to his covenant.

As the angels ascend and descend the staircase, there is a deep sense of the Lord's care for Jacob, that he will not let him down. It is no wonder that Jacob's response is to declare the awesomeness of the place and to name it Bethel, the house of God. In the third example, it is Hagar, the unfavoured slave girl of Sarah, who experiences seeing the Lord, hearing his promise of protection, and being given a promise of life for her and her son Ishmael and their descendants. She reflects, 'Have I really seen God and remained alive after seeing him?' (v.13). Thus she calls the spring where she has this unique encounter Beerlahairoi, which means 'the well of one who sees and lives'. This passage reveals that it is not always the most likely ones to whom God comes closest.

Such a reassuring theophany happened to Moses himself in Exodus 33:17–23. This came after the Israelites had made a golden calf image, revealing their seemingly endless disobedience, and the Lord's wrath was very great. He sent a plague upon them (32:35). The Lord promised forgiveness only because of Moses' faithfulness, and it was then that Moses asked the Lord to show him his glory. This is another way of asking for a direct vision of the Lord. Moses is then reminded that no one can see the Lord directly and live. What he is granted is a place within a cleft of the rock on Mount Horeb. From there he will be protected by the Lord's hand from seeing his face and so dying, but as he goes, Moses will be allowed to see his back, and will therefore live.

What is clear in all these passages is that there is no sense of freedom in terms of relationship with God. He may appear in blessing or otherwise, but it is at his choosing and control, it is a rare occurrence and one fraught with ambiguity. And he confines his appearances to special people, mainly patriarchs and prophets. It is only a chosen few who are given access to God, to his glory or his presence in storm, in still small voice or in a tent/tabernacle as they journey in the wilderness. And such encounters are deeply ambiguous experiences, full of awe as well as blessing. Such complexity continues into the period of entry into the promised land. Joshua is granted a theophany in terms very like those of Moses at the burning bush, as he

experiences a heavenly commander who assures him of the
Lord's support and tells him to take off his shoes, because he
is on holy ground in the Lord's presence (Joshua 5:13–15). The
ark travels with Joshua into Canaan, representing God's
presence with his people. At the same time, it is dangerous for
those not worthy to touch the ark and can lead to death (see 2
Samuel 6:7 and the death of Uzzah).

To return to our original passage, Exodus 19, the theophany
happens on a mountain. So often mountains are seen to be
places where God or gods live, and this is part of their mystery.
It is not surprising that Greek gods were said to live on Mount
Olympus. I climbed this mountain once and was struck by the
rocky remoteness of the peak, reached after many hours of
climbing along stony paths and through a high belt of dense
trees. There was a great ring of cloud around the top as I went
higher, but passing through that I came to an airy and deeply
atmospheric summit where it was easy to imagine the gods
dwelling. Another such dwelling place is the icy cave in the
mountains of Kashmir where Siva is said to have dwelt. Here
pilgrims used to go in droves at great personal cost, walking for
weeks, before the recent war intervened. In Ireland I remember
climbing Croagh Patrick in Galway, a place that has been
climbed much in holy pilgrimage. It is where St Patrick was
said to have gone to cast out all snakes from the emerald isle.
Today the walk is littered with cast-off shoes, some of them
with stiletto heels, which forced pilgrims to go barefoot.
Another such place is in the Cairngorms in Scotland, the most
remote of British mountains, where two of the great Everest
climbers recorded running away in terror one day from the
summit plateau of one of the peaks. They had experienced with
great vividness a presence beyond themselves, which induced
such a sense of fear even in these most experienced of mountain-
eers. The upper slopes of mountains can be such mysterious
places.

In Exodus 19 it is only the two mediators, Moses and Aaron,
who are granted the theophany, and after that the gift of the
Ten Commandments. The ordinary Israelites were not allowed
at first to 'touch the border of the mountain'. When they had

washed their clothes, and were sexually clean, then and only then could they come to the foot of the mountain and no further. There were all kinds of taboos preventing them having any direct contact with God. These related especially to purity. We can see here the beginning of a tradition that only special people, then priests, then eventually the high priest, could approach God in the holy of holies within his temple. The mountain here is like a prefiguring of the temple in Jerusalem with all its rules of access and exclusions.

So often religions are ringed round with such rules about approaching God. There is a holy mountain in Kerala, in south-west India, known as Sabaramalai. It is sacred to the Hindu god Ayappan, an increasingly popular South Indian deity, and each year there is a month of pilgrimage up the mountain. To qualify to make the pilgrimage devotees must abstain from all sexual relations, all alcohol, tobacco or drugs, they must wear black clothes and be unshaven, and must also be male or post-meno-pausal women. They must approach the top of the mountain without shoes, because of the polluting effect that it is con-sidered leather brings, in a religion where the cow is sacred.

Mainstream Hinduism is a religion which has developed all kinds of rules related to pollution. Caste and pollution are very much bound up together. To have any chance of salvation, according to some schools of thought, we must be reincarnated into a 'twice-born caste'. If possible, we must be a Brahmin, a member of the priestly caste which has unique access to God. Brahmins alone can enter the holy of holies in temples and perform the required rituals. At the other extreme, even the shadow of a Dalit, 'untouchable', is polluting. I visited a high-caste prisoner in the South Indian Jail in Madurai. He was there because he had killed a Dalit, whose leg had brushed the leg of his wife in a busy wedding crowd. In a major temple, like the Meenakshi Temple in Madurai, there is a large notice saying that only Hindus may go beyond a certain point. Gandhi fought to have this temple opened to 'Harijans' as he called Dalits, but there is no freedom of access to others who will also bring pollution.

Not all Hinduism of course is like this and some Bhakti

(devotional) movements in particular have opened up access to all castes. There is a story retold to me by a group of Dalits in a very poor village, a story which clearly meant a lot to them. A Dalit laboured in the fields of a Brahmin and wanted to go with his landlord to worship Natarajan (Siva) in the great temple at Chidambaram. But he was told he could not do so and should stick to his village gods. He was not worthy to go to a great temple, since he drank alcohol and sacrificed goats. He should rather get the harvest in, while his landlord travelled to Chidambaram. Miraculously the harvesting was done by Natarajan, and so the Brahmin reluctantly let the Dalit go with him. But there the Dalit could not worship because a stone bull (*nandi*, sacred to Siva) was in the way of his view from outside the temple. Here again Natarajan came to his aid. The bull miraculously moved a little to allow him to see. The Brahmins controlling the temple still would not let him enter. But he gazed from afar for fifteen days, and eventually the temple authorities relented and said he could enter if he could walk through fire. This he did and fell before his Lord, who then swallowed him up, except for his feet. This is a strong alternative tradition which suggests that the only true Brahmin is the one who is devout and fulfils their duty whatever their caste. This means that all potentially have access to God.

Nevertheless, even in Britain Dalits do not normally attend regular Hindu temples. They are permitted to, but prefer not to because so many centuries of history and taboos lie behind them. I was told by a group of Dalits in Birmingham that on one occasion in a temple one of their members had given out the *prasad* (sacred food) to the devotees in a service. When his background was discovered, it was made clear that this should never happen again.

With this experience around, it is not surprising that all other religions in India have benefited from those who have converted to them in protest against such a caste system and who have looked for a religion that would give free access to all. Buddhism, Sikhism, Islam and Christianity are all examples of this. The reality has frequently contradicted the theory, as further barriers are erected against the poor and those of low caste.

But, as an ideal at least, they are all egalitarian and all have equal access to God. I know a Brahmin convert to Christianity in London, and one of the catalysts for his decision was the experience he had of being given a sacred thread at the age of puberty, and being invited, because of his birth, to enter the sanctuary in his local temple. As he did so he saw a very good and elderly man of lower caste not allowed to go where he, a mere youth, was now taken because of his birth. He had always deeply admired this man's spirituality. The older man was barred for ever from going where he himself could go as a young upstart Brahmin with little understanding and no depth of belief. What was this religion about? Later he asked the same of Christianity, when this admired friend died and, by the rigid theology the Brahmin had converted to, would be forever excluded, as an unconverted Hindu, from the love of God.

The next section in Exodus, chapter 20, shows us another, more open side to God's relationship with his people. Here is one of the two versions of the Decalogue, the Ten Commandments, beginning in verse 2 with the assertion that God is the liberating one who has brought the Israelites out of Egypt. It is in response to that act of grace that they are challenged with keeping the commandments as their side of the covenant relationship. These instructions are for all, not for a special group of Jews. However, towards the end of the chapter (v.18ff.), the normal atmosphere of fear and trembling returns, as the people acknowledge the great gap between them and God and rely again on Moses as mediator. Their fear is of the kind of God portrayed in Psalm 18:8–16, with its graphic picture of God in his wrath. As the Bible record unfolds, the relationship between God and his people oscillates between these two poles. He is accessible through the Law he has given, and through the prophets and others who interpret his word or receive his Spirit. At the same time, he remains inscrutable and remote, both because of his nature and because of the fact that his people block him from them by the way they live their lives. Prayer and worship become the province of professionals, as the religion grows more cult- and ritual-dominated and temple-based.

God in the Old Testament is both remote and near, beyond their reach and yet deeply concerned with the affairs of the people of Israel. He is the judge and awesome one. Before him Job can only fall down and ask for mercy after all his questioning of God and the way God seems to have allowed him to suffer so unjustly. In chapters 38–41 God speaks directly to Job out of a whirlwind, which, as we have seen, signifies a theophany. He reveals himself as the creator God in all the wonderful manifestations of his creation, beautifully described in these chapters. It is not for Job to question but to fall before the Almighty One and ask for forgiveness. But this Almighty One is no longer the remote and anonymous God, but one who has spoken to him personally, one with whom he now has a relationship.

This same God is also the liberator God, the one who brings freedom to his people and is celebrated as such through much of the Bible. He is the God revealed in the prophet Hosea, with his portrayal of God's love for his people, especially in chapter 11, where God yearns for them like a mother for her child: 'When Israel was a child I loved him, and out of Egypt I called my son.' Yet, like a good parent, God gives them the freedom to go away: 'The more I called them, the more they went from me; they kept sacrificing to the Baals (Canaanite deities), and offering incense to idols.' This happened even though God had taught them to walk, and taken them in his arms, and led them with reins of love and compassion. They continually go away from him, but he cannot give them up: 'How can I give you up, Ephraim! How can I hand you over, O Israel! . . . my heart recoils within me, my compassion grows warm and tender' (v.8). Here is enacted before us the struggle between freedom and love in the relationship between Yahweh and his people.

All this is part of the underlying struggle to understand the mystery of God in his remoteness and almighty creative power, in his wrath and justice, and in his love, understanding and compassion.

We can see the same kind of struggle in Islam and its understanding of Allah. On the one hand, Allah is almighty and indescribable, remote and beyond understanding, the one before

whom Muslims can only fall in obeisance and servanthood.
This is the Allah of whom there can never be an image or a
picture, who can never be divided or compromised. As in the
case of Yahweh, he is the one whose thoughts are not our
thoughts and whose ways are not our ways. He is the one who
has absolute freedom, and will do as he wills, saving whom he
wills, having mercy on whom he wills and condemning whom
he wills. At the same time, the Qur'an also indicates that he is
'closer than our jugular vein'. He can be described with 99
beautiful names, which are wonderfully rich in their combined
feel: God is the agent, the restorer, the first and the last, he is
the wise and the watcher, the merciful, the compassionate, the
forgiver, the generous, the patient, the king, the governor. So
moved by this was a friend of mine that she wrote down 99
beautiful names for Jesus for her own meditation.

We turn now to the second passage, from the Epistle to the
Hebrews, chapter 12. This is a New Testament passage
unusually based quite closely on one from the Old Testament,
our first passage from Exodus 19. The writer of the epistle
contrasts the circumstances surrounding the rather terrifying
appearance of God at the time of the giving of the first covenant
with what is now possible through the second covenant. Then
even the chosen mediator, Moses, had exclaimed, 'I tremble
with fear,' and the mass of the people had been told, 'If even a
beast touches the mountain, it shall be stoned.' Now the writer
of the epistle assures his readers that they have come to the
sacred mountain, to Mount Zion, to heavenly Jerusalem. They
are already, in a sense, enrolled in heaven. The difference is
that Jesus is the mediator of this new covenant. As we have
seen from the rest of the epistle, he is the one who has gone
before us as the pioneer and perfecter of our faith. He is the one
who gives us access to God directly. It is no longer necessary to
encounter God through the high priest and through the sacrifice
of animals, for Jesus, the heir of all things through whom all
the world was created (1:2), has become the unrepeatable sacrifice on the cross and prepared the way for us to the heavenly
country. He has gone as the forerunner on our behalf (6:20),
having broken through the curtain separating humanity from

God (10:20). 'Consequently he is able for all time to save those who approach to God through him, since he always lives to make intercession for them' (7:25).

Through Jesus we can now approach God directly. No sacrifices are necessary, no building or person is necessary. We do not have to be of a particular birth or intellectual ability or of special piety or be perfect in character. The Jesus of the Epistle to the Hebrews is the one who is explicitly said to have sympathy with our weaknesses, and to have suffered with us and been tempted as we are (2:17–18, 5:15).

Jesus has promised to be with us in simple ways, and through Jesus God is present with us. He is there when two or three are gathered together in his name: he is there in the bread and wine of the Eucharist; he is there in the poor and the oppressed, the hungry and the thirsty, in the 'little ones'. In so far as we are helping these little ones, we are helping Jesus himself (Matthew 25:31–46).

We witness here a great freeing up of the way to God. If we look through the gospels, there is a special place for women, for sinners, for the poor and the blind, for those with leprosy, even for prostitutes. The Kingdom of God belongs potentially to all these people, and to all those who know their need of God. The parable of the Pharisee and the Publican is here of special importance. The publican who has not felt himself worthy even to enter the temple and prays from outside, 'God be merciful to me a sinner,' is the one who is 'justified' ('saved'), while the Pharisee who has done many good works, and knows it, is not commended. Jesus' entry to Jerusalem and cleansing of the temple was not just about money-changing, but about opening up access to the temple for prayer for people of all nations. This was to be the continuing battle that St Paul was to carry through as he gave his whole ministry to enabling Gentiles to become disciples of Jesus Christ without any manner of restrictions being placed upon them. His faith was that the cross and resurrection of Christ had opened the way for all, and that it was no longer a matter of whether someone was circumcised or not circumcised, whether they were Jew or Gentile. His deep conviction is that 'for freedom, Christ has set us free;

stand firm therefore, and do not submit again to a yoke of slavery' (Galatians 5:1).

Yet, though God frees us in Christ, so often we ourselves ring the mountain, the sanctuary, the altar, with our own taboos and restrictions. These often surround the Eucharist, the place of greatest openness, and yet often we make it the most restricted of sacraments. There is a story of an Italian painting of the Last Supper which boldly included women and a dog, besides the twelve disciples. The city fathers objected to the painting as being not a true replica of the Last Supper. The painter said he would rename it 'A meal in the house of Levi', if that would help. They said that would be fine, and he was able to display it!

Very often restrictions are about masculinity. This may relate to there being a male priest at the celebration, but it may on occasions be about the appropriateness of receiving the bread and wine. Even in the South Indian seminary where I taught, which has a radical reputation, women would often not receive the Eucharist when they were in the period of menstruation, reflecting the cultural taboo of the area. Probably we see here a mirror of the traditional Brahmin household, where the woman has to remain in a separate room at this time in the month and receive her food there. The blood is considered polluting. And this about a sacrament in Christ's blood for the forgiveness of sins!

Restrictions may relate to the perceived roles of priests and laity. In some churches a lay person will be very reluctant to enter the sanctuary even outside service times. I led a lay training weekend about the Holy Spirit in South India, and talked about freedom of the Spirit in worship. As a sign of this, I suggested that we should pass round the bread and wine to each other at the final Eucharist. This was a weekend for members of the United Church of South India, and it was the ex-Anglican members of that church, those who were most Eucharist-centred, who refused to take part. They said that only a priest could touch the chalice. I tried to enable them to feel free to take a risk at this point for the sake of the wider fellowship, but one of them said, 'My head understands what you are saying, but my feelings will not allow me.' It had been instilled in them through the teaching of clergy for so long that they could do certain things and not others.

Then there are our church restrictions on who can or cannot take the sacrament. Some churches restrict on the basis of denomination, others on the basis of age. Anglicans hold family Eucharists but often exclude children. People argue against their participation, stressing that children cannot understand. Yet this is the Body of a Christ who said the Kingdom of God belonged to children such as these, and instructed his disciples to let the children come to him. Do even the most sophisticated of adults ever understand this mystery anyway? A chaplain in a hospital for the mentally disabled said that his understanding of the Eucharist was transformed through leading a weekly service there. Where else do people say 'thank you' as they receive? John Wesley, who used to give the sacrament even to infants, remarked on the unusual awe that came upon them as they received. Some psychologists say that the time of greatest sensitivity to the imagination and to religious experience is at the age of eight or nine, and yet often that is before children are allowed access to the eucharistic sacrament, according to our rules.

I think here of the prison congregation I was involved with in India, which totalled about 60 and was two-thirds Hindu and one-third Christian. At the monthly Eucharist we used to give consecrated bread and wine only to baptised Christians, and, following the practice of the Orthodox Church, unconsecrated bread to Hindus. The sacrament of unity consequently became the sacrament of disunity. Two prisoners persuaded me to change the rules. One poor man, who was in prison for selling illegal alcohol to keep his family alive, longed to be baptised, but within the prison could not be because the rules precluded it. He also longed to take the Eucharist, but we said he should wait until he was baptised. He was released, and we began a period of preparation for him in his village, promising he would be baptised at Easter. He brought several others to the preparation class through his witness. Unfortunately, he suffered a haemorrhage before Easter. I baptised him on his deathbed in the hospital. He had been an evangelist for Christ, but had never been held 'worthy' to receive the body and blood of Christ.

Another man had killed someone in a village fight. Then he learned of a God who would forgive even him. He asked to take the bread and wine in the monthly service. I asked him why, and he said it was because he wished to feel truly forgiven. I told him that such a forgiveness was declared each week in whatever service we held. He said that he knew that but, 'Unless I kneel side by side with you, and receive from the same cup, I will not *feel* accepted.' Because of such cases, we opened up the Eucharist to 'all who love the Lord'. In arguing for this, I quoted from Jürgen Moltmann's book *The Open Church*, which argues that what needs to be justified is not every inclusion into the body of Christ but every exclusion. And so often, he says, we take exactly the opposite approach. Though I understand the complexity of the theological issues involved, dilemmas can be very sharp within our contemporary multi-religious society in Britain, where committed members of other faiths may wish to attend a Christian service, at least on an occasional basis, and that service is so often the Eucharist.

This does not happen, however, just with the Eucharist. How often do people feel they are not worthy to be in church, not respectable enough to be part of such a community! This happened traditionally to those, for example, who became pregnant outside marriage. In some restrictive communities in the last century they were even expelled publicly from the congregation. An example of a poignant exclusion is found within Thomas Hardy's tragic novel *Tess of the d'Urbervilles*.

Tess gives birth to a child out of wedlock, and the baby quickly falls terminally ill. Her father refuses to have the parson come to baptise the baby because of the shame the family would face. In desperate concern for the eternal soul of her son, Tess baptises him herself, naming him sadly 'Sorrow'. She concludes that 'if Providence would not ratify such an act of approximation, she, for one, did not value the kind of heaven lost by the irregularity – either for herself or for her child'. The child died, but even then she faced more sorrow from the church, as the parson, though behaving kindly and accepting that her approximation to baptism would count for God, felt unable to allow it to count for the Church, and refused her permission for a burial in consecrated ground. She had to bury her son outside that part of the churchyard, 'at the cost of a shilling and a pint of beer to the sexton, in that shabby corner of God's allotment where He lets nettles grow and where all unbaptised infants, notorious drunkards, suicides and others of the conjecturally damned are laid.' It seems that God is prepared to include Tess and her baby, but the parson and the Church are not. Maybe this would not happen today; there may have been some progress. But how much?

Some feel excluded, not by explicit restrictions, but by the culture they can sense surrounding the Church community. This often applies to young people, who are made to feel it is no place for them by the very people who will say there are no youth in the church. It may apply to those who feel they do not have the right clothes, or do not live in an appropriate kind of 'family', or are of the wrong sexual orientation.

In some churches people feel excluded because they do not fit in with a particular norm of prayer or spirituality. It may be that speaking in tongues is considered necessary, for example. If we lead worship, we may feel excluded because we do not know how to do things 'properly'. I remember as a child being a server of the sanctuary. The sacristan used to watch us from the back of the church, and I remember to this day his telling me that he was ashamed of me, because I had made one or two mistakes in the ritual required. I became afraid to go wrong. I remember the same feeling recurring at my theological college, as we led evening prayer in front of our fellows and staff. Far from feeling free, I felt incredibly constricted lest I make a mistake. The same can happen to those who lead the Eucharist; it can be immensely enabling and freeing, or it can become a block to the movement of the Spirit, so strictly do certain conventions have to be adhered to.

There is a story of a group of islanders who were visited by a missionary in the South Pacific Islands. He stayed with them for some time, and they wished to know more about how to approach the God he taught them of. He spent many hours teaching them the Lord's Prayer and they struggled to memorise it. Eventually he tested them and they got it right all through. This was in the evening, and he said he would therefore move on the next day, his job done. The next morning they escorted him to his boat, and as he set off, he shouted to them to repeat the prayer. They began correctly, but then got completely lost. In the end, one of them cried out, 'God loves us, and we love him, and we are happy!' He smiled as they tried so hard, and shouted back, 'Feel free, pray to God in your own way, he loves you as you are.'

Sadly, as the Gospel was spread from Europe in the colonial period, there went with it much of the European way of doing things. In many of the ex-Anglican churches of Tamilnadu, even 50 years after the formation of the United Church, the true way to worship God is seen as that set out in the Book of Common Prayer of 1662. Along with this should go European hymns translated into Tamil, rather than lyrics and popular songs in the indigenous idiom. Worship should also take place in a European-style building such as those found in the south of England, if possible with a spire or tower, and such places are still being built. Candles should be used and not Indian lamps, the organ played and not local drums or, even worse, the flute, which is seen as associated with Hinduism because it is said to have been played by Krishna.

In Zimbabwe I experienced in the same congregation both the discipline of a European-style service in English, and the remarkable exuberance of an all-night prayer meeting around the body of a congregation member who had died. The former expressed one way of worship and was well done, but the latter was where the heart was released and people were able to be themselves, as they shared in dance and rhythm, song and testimony, with the widow and her family. Here we came to understand much about the communion of saints and of the place of ancestors in the world view of the congregation members. Here there was no barrier between lay and ordained, or between men and women, as all 'had access to the Father in the one Spirit'.

Perhaps another example of the challenge to be free is in the area of inclusive language, particularly in relation to our prayer to God. For some there will never be any wish to address God as mother. The fatherhood of God has never been a problem theologically or in terms of worship. For others today this is clearly not so, and the expression of the motherhood of God alongside fatherhood has become important. In this context of freedom, it seems sad that either of these groups should put pressure upon the other: that you must address God as mother as well as father, or that you must not address God as mother.

The offer in Jesus Christ is to be free before God, free in the Spirit in the deepest sense. In Romans 8:26, Paul shows us that we cannot go wrong in prayer: 'The Spirit helps us in our weakness; for we do not know how to pray as we ought, but the Spirit himself intercedes for us with sighs too deep for words.' As we have seen in John 4, what matters is sincerity and truth, not 'the right way of doing things'. Of course, this is not a licence to be sloppy and ill-prepared in worship or prayer – in that way our worship would cease to be in sincerity or in truth. But how we do it becomes less important.

I personally would add 'freedom' to the words of Jesus about worship being in Spirit and in truth. True worship is in Spirit, in truth and in freedom. That freedom includes the freedom to say 'thank you' in prayer. Though our books often suggest that intercessions and thanksgivings should come together in the Eucharist, how often this part of the service seems to be a list of problems and prayer for them. How rarely do we hear a prayer of thanksgiving! Yet Meister Eckhart wisely said, 'If the only prayer you say in your whole life is thank you, then that would suffice.' This freedom includes the freedom to forgive and be forgiven, to understand that we are accepted by God as we are, not as we feel guilty for not being. This freedom includes the freedom to be still, 'to be still and know that I am God'. So often we rush in our daily life from experience to action, experience to proclamation. We leave out the stillness and reflection in between, and yet that so often gives us the space and freedom to move on.

This freedom is about the freedom to offer our language, culture and tradition in worship and prayer. I experienced this happening wonderfully in the great worship tent in Harare for the fiftieth anniversary assembly of the World Council of Churches in 1998. Over the duration of the assembly, there was a marvellous balance between discipline and freedom in worship, and the best from all the major cultures was offered, as well as the variety of languages and church traditions. Here, above all in the assembly, we felt free to be ourselves, amidst all the words, resolutions and activism of everything else that went on. I found this freedom in the chapel of the United College of the Ascension, Selly Oak. Sometimes the Eucharist seemed a prefiguring of the Kingdom of God, particularly when the Lord's Prayer was said by each in his or her own language, and there were usually 20 or more at any one time.

So it is also on Ascension Day, when the words of the gospel, 'I will be with you always, till the end of time,' are read in so many different languages. There is a feeling both of the pride each has in using their mother tongue, and truly the universality of the text, which has indeed been preached to all nations. This must have seemed a mere pipe dream, on that barren Galilean mountaintop, when it was expressed to eleven frightened disciples, 'some of whom doubted'. There is a real freedom in the Spirit in the combination of so many much-loved languages. There is harmony in the disharmony. It was the same when someone prayed in their own language in the chapel; such a prayer had a freedom and joy that can rarely come in a second language.

I began this meditation with a mountain, one both of threat and in the end of promise. God in his remoteness there addressed Moses. I end with another mountain, that of the Transfiguration. Three disciples are given a vision of the eternal Christ, of the resurrected Lord (Matthew 17:1–13). They also learn that the same Lord is also the suffering one, and that these two experiences must go together. Peter likes the one and not the other. But overall, the Transfiguration experience is one of freedom for these chosen disciples. Their eyes transcend the normal limitations of sight, their minds become unclouded, their ears become unstopped, and they see Jesus as he really is. It is an experience they receive rather than earn. It is the ultimate in access to God that is possible on this earth.

This happened only to the three senior disciples. But after the resurrection, all of them find themselves opened to such an experience in their encounters with the risen Lord. At Pentecost, such possibilities are given to all who were present in Jerusalem, in a great outpouring of the Spirit, and the promise is given 'for you, for your children and for all who are far away, everyone whom the Lord our God calls to him' (Acts 2:39). There is here a great democratisation of the Spirit, as prophesied by the prophet Joel: 'I will pour out my Spirit upon all flesh, and your sons and your daughters shall prophesy, your young men shall see visions, and your old men shall dream dreams. Even on my slaves, both men and women, in those days I will pour out my Spirit' (2:17–18). Today's readers are included in that bestowal of the Spirit; we are those who are far off in time and in distance. No less than those gathered in Jerusalem at that first Pentecost, we all have access to the Father in the One Spirit.

Perhaps the key result of all this is found in a new centrality in love, expressed most clearly in 1 John 4, where the writer tells us that God is love, and that the one who abides in love abides in God, and God abides in that person. This means (v.18) that there is no fear in love, for perfect love casts out fear. It is this end to fear in our relationship with God that brings us freedom in worship and prayer. This passage indicates the long journey travelled since Moses encountered God on the mountain.

Readers' response

- In stillness, relax the body and mind and feel free before God. Be open to receiving him in any way that he may come to you.

- Think about what blocks you from being free before God. What are the clouds, taboos or restrictions that hinder your prayer life? What of the worship life of your church?

- Feel free to overflow with thanksgiving for what God has done for you in your life and name at least three of those things.

- Make a list of your own beautiful names for Jesus – at least a dozen, if not 99! Then meditate on them: 'Jesus my friend, Jesus my brother . . .'

Passages for meditation

Dietrich Bonhoeffer, 'The Old Testament and the New'; a letter from Tegel prison, written on the Second Sunday in Advent 1943, *Letters and Papers from Prison*, pp.136–7:

> My thoughts and feelings seem to be getting more and more like those of the Old Testament, and in recent months I have been reading the Old Testament much more than the New. It is only when one knows the unutterability of the name of God that one can utter the name of Jesus Christ; it is only when one loves life and the earth so much that without them everything seems to be over that one may believe in the resurrection and a new world; it is only when one submits to God's law that one may speak of grace; and it is only when God's wrath and vengeance are hanging as grim realities over the heads of one's enemies that something of what it means to love and forgive them can touch our hearts. In my opinion it is not Christian to want to take our thoughts and feelings too quickly and too directly from the New Testament. We have already talked about this several times, and every day confirms my opinion. One cannot and must not speak the last word before the last but one. We live in the last but one and believe the last, don't we?

Henri Nouwen, *Bread for the Journey*, p.391:

> At some moments we experience complete unity within us and around us. This may happen when we stand on a mountaintop and are captivated by the view. It may happen when we witness the birth of a child or the death of a friend. It may happen when we have an intimate

conversation or a family meal. It may happen in church during a service or in a quiet room during prayer. But whenever it is or however it happens we say to ourselves: 'This is it . . . everything fits . . . all I ever hoped for is here.'

This is the experience that Peter, James and John had on the top of Mount Tabor when they saw the aspect of Jesus' face change and his clothing become sparkling white. They wanted that moment to last forever (see Luke 9:28–36). This is the experience of the fullness of time. These moments are given to us so that we can remember them when God seems far away and everything seems empty and useless. These experiences are true moments of grace.

Chapter 4

FREEING OTHERS TO BE THEMSELVES

John 21:15–23

> When Peter saw him, he said to Jesus, 'Lord, what about him?' Jesus said, 'If it is my will that he remain until I come what is that to you? Follow me!'
>
> *John 21:21–2*

In the middle of the Muslim fasting month of Ramadan, I led a small group of Christians on a visit to our local mosque, to break the fast with the Muslims at the end of the day. We had decided to fast and to use the Advent prayer intention of peace with justice in Afghanistan, where war was raging. It was a moving occasion to eat dates and drink rose milk with seven hundred Muslims. At the end we engaged in informal dialogue for half an hour. One of the Muslims I know addressed me as 'Brother Andrew' and stated that God wanted there to be only one religion in the world and that must be the last one that was to supplant all others. It was self-evidently Islam! I smiled and suggested this was not how I saw things. He smiled back, and my friend the imam said to the zealous evangelist, 'Let Andrew be, you won't convert him!' We all laughed, and continued to talk of other things, our friendship uninterrupted. We differ, and will always expect to do so, but our friendship continues out of mutual respect and the ability to let each other be himself. This same imam has written in a dialogue with me in our diocesan magazine: 'I know that Andrew would like me to be a Christian, and I would like him to be Muslim. This

is extremely unlikely to happen, and so meanwhile, we live in
friendship with each other and learn from each other.'

Allowing others to be themselves does not prevent me being
myself. It is because the imam has said, I give you space to be
with us as a Christian, that I feel free to be myself, as I relate
to him, without hidden agendas or manipulation. It does not
mean that I must let go of my grasp of truth to be in this
relationship; I am accepted as a whole person, including my
beliefs. We meet as Ibrahim and Andrew, not as Islam and
Christianity, or as Indian Muslim and the Church of England.
We meet with all our strengths and our weaknesses, our
respective senses of humour and a growing sense of trust.
Indeed we can sometimes share things with each other that
assume confidentiality without saying this formally. This friendship is rooted in a tacit understanding that we each allow the
other to be himself, and that we make no attempt to control or
manipulate each other.

Such an acceptance is not common between people of two
different faiths, amongst whom the norm has been attitudes of
superiority, rejection and often hostility. The sense of common
humanity which God created us with is overshadowed or obliter-
ated by religious or theological walls which refuse to accept
that others choose to think or live differently, whether we like
it or not. Such an acceptance goes further when we come to
realise that the other person is what they are, not in spite of
their not being of the same faith as myself, but because of the
way they live that other faith.

Sutadhara is a Buddhist monk from Sri Lanka. As Principal
of the United College of the Ascension in Selly Oak, Birmingham, I suggested an annual scholarship for someone of
another faith. Our two sponsors, the Anglican missionary
society USPG and the Methodist Church, agreed to finance this.
The requirement was that visiting interfaith fellows should be
themselves, and wish to learn from Christians as themselves.
Sutadhara wore his saffron robes, allowing himself the luxury
of a cardigan, and became a central member of the multi-
national community. He discovered the game 'pool', and was
seen to take on all comers in the common room. He attended

classes on the Psalms, on 1 Corinthians, and my Bible study group. As we read the story of the institution of the Eucharist, and were asked to offer responses, it was only Sutadhara who highlighted the social obligations towards the poor, which are a requirement of a true Eucharist. In the Bible study group we were each asked to interpret to the others a parable which spoke to us. Sutadhara shared a powerful story of the Buddha. Gradually he won the hearts of the community.

He attended a debate on Christian approaches to people of other faiths. Some of the theologies expressed had the implication of ruling him decisively out of heaven, and a minority even consigned him to worse. I asked him afterwards whether he found the evening difficult. 'No,' he said with the twinkle he often had in his eye. 'I really enjoy hearing Christians argue with each other!' It was with such a sense of generosity that he responded to what I felt was a real rejection.

It was arranged that he should lead a period of meditation one morning for the colleges. Sadly, some Christians, both staff and students, from another college did not attend, feeling that this was not an appropriate thing for them to do. Sutadhara led us in a beautiful meditation on loving compassion, for ourselves, for our families, our friends, those to whom we are indifferent, our enemies, and the whole of creation. He told us to be ourselves, and to meditate as we would, focusing on Jesus the compassionate and crucified one, as he focused on the Buddha. At the end, he said that he knew it was our custom to say the grace, and asked if one of us would lead the group in offering that prayer. I reflected upon a sculpture I had seen in a monastery in mountainous forests near Kyoto in Japan. It had been placed in the centre of the meditation room and depicted the Buddha in dialogue with Jesus, impossible in history, but something being enacted before our eyes, as we encountered each other, a disciple of the Buddha and disciples of Jesus.

My wife and I recently made a short visit to Sri Lanka. We were determined to find time to visit our friend Sutadhara. He received us and our Sri Lankan Christian travelling companions with unfeigned joy, and we embraced each other as brothers across culture and religion. He revealed that he had been recently in a major road accident. He had broken his leg in three places, and had been in hospital for several weeks. He remarked how good it was to be in hospital when you are an interfaith person: 'I have received visits, blessings and prayers from the Anglican bishop, from Hindus and Muslims, as well as from my fellow Buddhist monks! That is why my leg is recovering so quickly!' We shared a delicious meal given by his Muslim neighbours, when he asked me to serve him, since a monk should not serve himself! He asked me to offer a prayer of grace. I felt in a way that that meal had a truly eucharistic feel, based on a willingness for each of us to be ourselves and to allow the others to be themselves.

Another Buddhist I knew well was Fuengsin.[1] She was from Thailand, married to an English Roman Catholic. We were co-teachers of Dialogue. She had no special academic qualifications, but was the best and most humorous teacher of Buddhism that I have known, as well as being a kind and gentle personality. She fell ill with stomach cancer. Very short in stature, she seemed to shrink rapidly before our eyes. Admitted to hospital, she meditated early each morning before her household Buddha, at the end of her bed in a public ward. Her student son was visiting one day when I was present. He asked if he could pray for her, but did not know the words to use. She took his hand, put it on her stomach, and said, 'Pray for me in the name of Jesus!' This released us both to be ourselves. She died shortly afterwards in a Roman Catholic hospice. She asked that I and a Hindu friend be present when her monks came from London to tend her on her deathbed, to perform the last rites, to enable her to surrender 'to the *dharma*'. Her bed was moved to the chapel, and rested under a picture of Jesus with open arms on the cross. As we waited for the monks to arrive, I felt moved to read the 23rd Psalm with her husband, knowing how she always encouraged us to be ourselves. When they came, they brought a statue of the Buddha, flowers and holy water. Where should they put them? The only place was the altar table. I told them to place them there. I felt the Jesus above them would want them to be themselves. As they chanted their rituals and asked her to surrender, I felt in a strange way that the Jesus above us was accepting her as she was, with his open arms, not in spite of her Buddhism, but with her faithfulness through death and beyond. It was a theological conundrum, but at her funeral a few days later I had no hesitation in reading 1 Corinthians 13, since her life seemed to mirror such a love.

Because she was free to be herself, she blossomed like a scented flower or a lotus, whose fragrance enriched our lives greatly, as described in this passage from one of the Pali scriptures, the Dhammapada:

52   As a flower that is lovely, beautiful and scent-laden, even so fruitful is the well-spoken word of one who practises it.

53   As from a heap of flowers, many a garland is made, even so many good deeds should be done by one born a mortal.

54   The perfume of flowers blows not against the wind, nor does the fragrance of sandal-wood, tagara and jasmine; but the fragrance of the virtuous blows against the wind; the virtuous person pervades every direction.

58, 59 As upon a heap of rubbish thrown on the highway, a sweet-smelling, lovely lotus there may grow, even so amongst the rubbish of beings, a disciple of the Fully Enlightened One outshines the blind wordlings with wisdom.

I have written so far about cross-faith freedom, for each to be themselves across faiths. But what of those relationships which are with us day to day? These include those closest to us – our children, our parents, our siblings, our spouses. Only these last have we chosen. They include our friends, those we have chosen to spend time with. They include our neighbours and work colleagues, whom we have probably not chosen. They include those to whom we are indifferent, and those whom we feel a natural hostility towards or who we feel are hostile to us. They include those of other cultures or races, whom we perhaps do not understand. These webs of relationships make up our world and contribute to who we become. We live too in relationship to the environment, God's creation, living and inanimate. How can we envelop all of these in a relationship of responsible freedom, where we allow each to be themselves, in relation to ourselves and to others? In terms of these circles of concern, I think of Sutadhara's range of meditation mentioned above, and how as Christians they all become enveloped in God's love. Perhaps where this may be easiest is in the circles in the middle distance from us; where it is hardest is often with those who are nearest and those who are farthest away.

Parents often find it very difficult to give freedom to their children. The freedom to make their own way in their own time is something children claim, but it is hard to give. Parents can at the same time be proud of the way their children are growing up, and yet want to avoid the consequence of this for themselves, the requirement that they begin to let go. If they do not offer this freedom, they will face revolt, either open or through deceit, and endless battles. They may also harm the very relationship central to them, so that trust is very hard to regain. Permanent damage to the relationship may be done, or it may take years to repair. Such growth towards independence is now taking place at a much younger age. My headmaster and my father insisted that I specialise in Latin and Greek, rather than maths, in the years leading to GCE (as it was then). This was 40 years ago. Now, such pressure would be hard to countenance, and would lead in most cases to the digging in of heels and revolt. Western culture encourages freedom of choice at an increasingly younger age, and to be able to make such choices is a sign of growing maturity, being responsible for our own development. Such independence was not of such central importance in the traditional family, nor is it so in many Asian cultures today.

Therefore, the challenge to give our children the freedom to be themselves has become all the sharper, at the same time as the world in some ways seems a harsher place. It may not actually be so, but the media's exposure of the dangers facing our growing children and teenagers is now widespread. The challenge is how to offer freedom without opting out of our proper role as parents: how to be available as guides, to enable our children to know that they are loved unconditionally, to provide always the open

arms that will receive them back if things have gone wrong and
they need a haven of peace and support. It is also about when
on extreme occasions to act as police or custodians, when the
dangers are so overwhelming that responsibility requires us to
change roles.

We have probably heard read at baptisms or weddings an
evocative extract from *The Prophet* by Kahlil Gibran, a book
published no fewer than 40 times between 1926 and 1988, as
this mystical and evocative Lebanese Muslim writer speaks across
the generations:

> And a woman who held a babe against her bosom said,
>   Speak to us of Children.
> And he said:
> Your children are not your children.
> They are the sons and daughters of Life's longing for itself.
> They come through you but not from you,
> And though they are with you yet they belong not to
>   you.
> You may give them your love but not your thoughts,
> For they have their own thoughts.
> You may house their bodies but not their souls,
> For their souls dwell in the house of tomorrow,
> Which you cannot visit, not even in your dreams.
> You may strive to be like them, but seek not to make them
>   like you.
> For life goes not backward nor tarries with yesterday.
> You are the bows from which your children as living arrows
>   are sent forth.
> The Archer sees the mark upon the path of the infinite,
>   and He bends you with His Might that His arrows
>   may go swift and far.
> Let your bending in the Archer's hand be for gladness:
> For even as He loves the arrow that flies, so He loves also
>   the bow that is stable.

I read this as part of my sermon at my mother's funeral. She had
probably never read the poem, but her way of being mother

had been very like this. Her four children had all gone their various ways, made their choices for good and their mistakes. They had ended up very different one from another. But she had always been there, allowing us the freedom to be ourselves, and as 'the bow that is stable', ready to receive us back, and to give support whenever we asked for it. We knew her love was there, whether we asked for it or not. She had never travelled outside the British Isles, and she was the last of our relatives that we would have expected to travel to India when we were there. Yet none of the more likely candidates came, they all made excuse. My wife and I were suffering from hepatitis at the same time, and were amazed to get a telegram to say that she was coming. It was a cure in itself to see her arrival on the small local plane, carrying overweight hand-luggage gifts for us in Marks & Spencer green bags, just as if she were coming from her local shop. There when we needed it, the bow that is strong. Though our being in India had little parallel with the journey away from home taken by the Prodigal Son, nor, I hope, had we 'wasted our substance', nevertheless my mother coming out to meet us so totally unexpectedly and offering us, in those bags, 'the fatted calf' reminded me of the father in that much-loved story and his overwhelming generosity.

The need to let those closest to us be themselves applies to all our relationships. I am aware that my sister and I still play out the same games with each other in our fifties that we did in our teens. As the dominant elder brother, I tried to exert control then. She grew up to be assertive in response, something I have never really accepted. And so the sibling rivalry remains. Now we can joke about it, as we each try to control the other. We still find it difficult to accept that I am myself and she is herself.

My eldest daughter, Joanna, had a major stroke at the age of twenty. Out of the blue, with no prior warning or diagnosable cause, she was struck down. She lost all her power of speech and movement on her right side, all her knowledge of maths, all her foreign languages, and her sense of grammar in English. It has taken her 11 years to make nearly a full recovery. From the beginning she asserted her right to be herself, not to be protected unnecessarily. Her sense of independence could be infuriating, as she struggled to be the age she was, when she should have flown the nest, at the same time as needing her parents desperately for all kinds of things. At first she was in a wheelchair, living in a rehabilitation centre. One day I came to see her and found she was reading a copy of *New Musical Express*. I asked her how she got it, and she said someone had wheeled her the half-mile to get it from the newsagent. The next week she had the same paper. I asked who had wheeled her. Proudly she said no one, but that she had got out of her chair and pushed it along the street, as her support, and bought the paper. I still remember her look of satisfaction. She was grasping the freedom to be herself, and we had to give her that space, with all the risks involved, because only in that way could she grow. She has never returned to live at home, but again and again we have had to find her rooms that she has chosen, often in places we would rather she was not going to live. She has made choices in her life that have not, we have felt, always been the right ones, but they have been her choices. We have had to learn the hard way when to act for her, when to make her act, and when to back off as she has claimed the freedom due to her age. At these points, she was not someone recovering from a stroke, but a young woman in her twenties.

A key point in her progress came when she asked out of the blue to return to her childhood home of South India. She had never wished to go with the rest of us in earlier times. Others asked how we could let her go on her own; she asked us only at short notice, when we ourselves were about to go on holiday. We could have made excuses. But we moved all things to get a ticket. We arranged contacts for her to stay with, but she first chose to go to an ecological project she had seen advertised in London. This was the one part that did not work out, since it turned out to be a bogus way of making money out of foreign young people. We had to refrain from saying that we had told her so. She travelled around South India, increasingly making her own arrangements, adjusting them from what we had arranged from England through friends, and gently asserting her independence from those we had arranged to 'protect' her. I saw a changed person when I met her at Heathrow. She showed me her diary, and it contained these words: 'I have been happier in India than I have been for years. The pace of life is so much more accepting.' It is from that point that she has, in her own words, looked forward and not back, and a new acceptance of herself has come, with positive decisions taken about her future and an increased confidence about taking control of her own life.

The hardest relationship, perhaps, to allow space to the other to be themselves, is that between two people who have chosen each other in marriage or other form of partnership. Two people are perhaps attracted to each other because they are different from each other, and their characteristics seem complementary. Such differences can become irritations or worse when things grow difficult. Then it can easily become a battle to see who can control the other. If this is not resolved in time, either the partnership breaks or they can begin to live alongside each other but not with each other. Areas of friction can be manifold. They may centre on who makes decisions, as one partner tries to control every decision, at first perhaps only the large ones, but then every small decision – how they will spend their leisure time, where they will go for their holidays, which friends they will ask, what they will buy when they go shopping, what film they will go to, how the house will be furnished, what TV programme they will watch, what they will have for supper, whether they will go to church or not. We can all write our own list.

There may also be a tussle to change the other's personality. Complementarity can become mutual destruction. If we know our personality profiles (as, for example, assessed through the Myers-Briggs analysis mentioned earlier), we may find one person imposing on the other. The extrovert does not respect the need of the introvert for space to regain his/her energy, but always wants people around. The introvert wants to shut others out. The intuitive partner has grand and often impractical ideas, while the other can appear to pour cold water, as he/she appears obsessed by detail. One partner seems always to want to go with the flow, adjust plans continually on the whim of the moment, and disregard time, while the other needs to know what is happening in detail, finds change difficult, and expects things to be punctual. The first type can be infuriating, as they always seem to give the impression that their apparently more exciting personality is always right, and that the other is a stick-in-the-mud who is always putting a brake on things. Quoting the kind of personality we are may become very annoying to the other, as it becomes an excuse for not doing what we do not want to do.

If we can rejoice in each other's differences, on the other hand, we can become a strong team. The rough edges are rubbed off. We each become less extreme in the manifestation of our preferences, and begin to let go of what may in itself have become a burden of expectation – to act up to our profile. To be able to feel that it does not matter if we do not succeed, are not always prominent, can enjoy spending time on our own or with one other person, can be liberating. The other can give us that freedom as a precious gift. And vice versa, as the other begins to relax about matters of detail and accept that things do not have to be perfect. We can enjoy laughing at each other's obsessions, and set each at liberty to enjoy our differences.

Again, from *The Prophet,* on marriage:

> Love one another, but make not a bond of love:
> Let it rather be a moving sea between the shores of your
>   souls.
> Fill each other's cup but drink not from one cup.
> Give one another of your bread but eat not from the same
>   loaf.
> Sing and dance together and be joyous, but let each one
>   of you be alone,
> Even as the strings of a lute are alone though they quiver
>   with the same music.
> Give your hearts but not into each other's keeping.
> For only the hand of Life can contain your hearts.
> And stand together yet not too near together:
> For the pillars of the temple stand apart,
> And the oak tree and the cypress grow not in each other's
>   shadow.

This is easy to affirm on the wedding day when the passage is sometimes read. But the shadows so often grow darker and darker

over those who have pledged to give each other space. Two
extracts from the love letters of Gibran to Mary Haskell underline
this message:[2]

> Marriage doesn't give any rights in another person except
> such rights as that person gives – nor any freedom except the
> freedom which that person gives.

> The surest basis for marriage is friendship – the sharing of
> real interests – the ability to fight out ideas together and
> understand each other's thoughts and dreams.

The same dynamic can happen in those who work with each
other. If they understand each other's strengths and meet each
other halfway, a team can be very effective. If the members are
consciously or subconsciously thinking, 'Why can't the others
be like me?' then the team will not be a happy place to be. I
once worked with a colleague whom I greatly respected, and vice
versa. However, for her I had the infuriating habit of changing
meetings and plans, for what I was convinced was the greater
need at the time. She would dig her heels in, and I would find
myself nearly always giving way, even when I felt she was
being completely unreasonable – for example, about changing a
meeting between the two of us weeks ahead. I would give way
and be left feeling resentful. One day I found myself refusing to
make this adjustment. I asserted that she was being unreasonable,
rather than me being over-flexible. To my surprise, she burst into
tears, something I had never seen before. I won this particular
skirmish. But more important, this was a breakthrough in our
working together. We began to laugh at each other's differences
and to see that they were together a strength, if we could adjust
a bit one to the other. Both of us had to be willing to act out of
our shadow, and could after some time rejoice in doing this and
found it easier. A third person was added to the team, with
another set of strengths and weaknesses, and we were able to use
this experience to find the addition easy to adjust to, and the
three of us together became more than the three of us as
individuals, once we had freed each other to be ourselves.

Part of the secret of maintaining such relationships and to

enable mutual creativity can lie, suggests the Jesuit spiritual writer Max Olivia, in learning to say what he calls 'the freedom prayer'. He learned this from finding himself deeply jealous of his fellow brothers who were developing friendships with those whom he thought saw him as the centre of their relationships with the order. He was advised by his spiritual director to pray for *freedom from the need to be special.* He writes:[3]

> As I practised this form of prayer, I began to realise that I was not praying never to be treated in a special way again. Over that we have no control. A key word is 'need', the *need* to be special. What is healed is the unfreedom. Thus one gradually becomes free and is at peace whether one is treated specially or not.

Olivia has a particular problem which he manages to name, the difficulty of allowing someone in his community not to show interest in him, though he himself was always listening to this person:

> I began asking myself: *What do I need that this man is not giving me?* And I saw what it was: interest. He had no interest in me. So I applied the freedom-prayer. Every time I felt this spirit of resentment rising, or caught myself in it after the fact, I prayed for freedom from the need for him to be interested in me. Gradually the feeling of resentment diminished and I was able to be present to the man in a loving way.

Such issues apply also to Christian congregations. It applies between clergy and lay people. Often clergy do not free their lay people or their congregations to be themselves, in all their variety and possibility. They have fixed ideas about how the laity should be – often a mirror of themselves – and so inhibit their growth. They become 'God's frozen people'. Educationally, they teach their congregations what they feel is the truth, rather than enable them to discover the truth together. The Bible becomes a source of statements to be followed, rather than a place of inspiration which can be studied together. Learning becomes minimal, though people spend a long time in church listening or go to

Bible study groups where again they only receive. The situation is described graphically in John Hull's seminal study *What Prevents Christian Adults Learning?*[4]

It is this situation that has been addressed by the Base Community movement in Latin America. Returned to the people, the Bible became the source of radical change. With a World Council of Churches Delegation, I once attended a Bible study in Nicaragua. Most of the participants were women, few had more than minimal school qualifications. But the dynamic of that morning was unforgettable for all of us highly theologically qualified observers. Here were a group of women freed by the process and by the enabler to own the scriptures for themselves, freed to relate them to the realities of their lives of struggle.

Such a dynamic has been found historically wherever movements of empowerment have taken place. It was found in the mass conversion movements amongst the Dalit peoples of India, as they discovered that though history had made them into crushed, marginal and untouchable people, that was not how God had created them. They were enabled to find freedom both in the spiritual message of liberation in Christ, and also in being led to take the concrete steps needed to free themselves from the chains of casteism at a local level. In the process three types of Dalit theology arose – theology *about* Dalits, theology *for* Dalits, and theology *by* Dalits. This latter was the fruit of full freedom, where they were given the space, or took the space, to reflect on the Gospel in their own terms, not as delivered to them by others. Here they grasped for themselves the egalitarian potency of the Gospel and what it could mean to their lives. It is to them as the powerless poor, rather than to them as sinners, that such a Gospel gave liberation to be themselves.

The dynamic has been found in recent times in what has become known as 'post-colonial hermeneutics'.[5] This movement looks at who has the voice, from whose perspective the Bible is read. It tries to enable those from the underside, those who are normally silent or marginalised, to have a voice: 'It provides a location for other voices, histories and experiences to be heard.' 'It is an act of reclamation, redemption and reaffirmation,' bringing out parts of the text that have been passed over or

forgotten, in the interests of the powerful. It allows the excluded
to have a voice, to be free to be heard. In this sense, a parallel
is found in women's reading of scripture. Texts have been there
for two millennia, but suddenly they can be seen in a new way,
as we are freed to read them from the perspective of women as
a marginalised community. Reading of texts such as the Haemo-
rrhaging Woman (Mark 5:25–34), the Syrophoenician Woman
(Mark 7:24–34), and the Anointing Woman (Mark 14:3–9) for
example, are drawn upon by the Japanese theologian Hisako
Kinukawa; examples of 'resistance for all these women', so
that they 'may experience life-communion with Jesus'. These
encounters were freeing both for Jesus and for the women to be
themselves. They were reciprocal and both sides received and
learned something, as the women challenged purity, ethnic
and sexual barriers.

It was found, in Britain, in a working-class parish in Sheffield,
when the priest, Alan Ecclestone, introduced the church meeting
as the centre of the life of the local congregation. Here all were
welcome, here the congregation as the Body of Christ was fully
incarnate. Issues of church and community were engaged with
in the light of Bible and theology, to enable the possibility of
change, and above all to free each to be a participant and not an
observer. What was key here was the fact that the priest, very
able as he was, committed himself to stay decades and not years
in that place. He would be alongside them in the decisions they
took, and himself follow through the consequences, rather than
move out when the going got difficult.

Lay people, of course, sometimes put unbearable pressure on
clergy to be what they want them to be. They prevent them being
what God has made them, but try to remake them in their own
image, so that they are not disturbed. They prevent the clergy
from being free to lead and gradually their energy and creativity
become drained in their impossible struggle to please. They are
forced to act out of character and end up neither being satisfied
themselves nor satisfying those they are serving. Clergy too often
look over their shoulders to those in the next parish or beyond.
They do not accept that each is different with different gifts to
offer, but they can become frozen with envy for the gifts of

others, whether fellow clergy or laity. They can become like Peter in John 21. He was affirmed by Jesus three times as the one who is to feed his sheep, because of the love Peter had expressed. He is also told that he would die a death which would glorify God but would not be of his choosing. But rather than becoming freed by this from the guilt induced by his earlier threefold denial of his Lord, he turns to the beloved disciple, who is nearby, and asks what is going to happen to him. He is told that that is nothing to do with him, even if the beloved disciple is to remain until Jesus comes. Jesus wants to free Peter to be himself, not to allow him to spend time speculating on what is to happen to others.

In the biblical narrative, Jesus faced much murmuring because his disciples were not John the Baptist's disciples. John and Jesus were different, so were their disciples. Each freed the other to be themselves, within the overall calling to respond to their vocation under God. John's disciples fasted and kept the rules; Jesus' disciples feasted and lived in a different way. So also with John and Jesus: 'John came neither eating nor drinking, and they say, "He has a demon"; the Son of Man came eating and drinking and they say, "Look, a glutton and a drunkard, a friend of tax gatherers and sinners" ' (Matthew 11:18–19). This points to the essence of Jesus' ministry – to eat with others as a sacrament of inclusion. Such meals were feasts of freedom, as barriers were broken down in mutual acceptance.

The President of the Methodist Conference in 2000–2001, Inderjit Boghal, a minister of Sikh background, who knows much himself about the breaking down of barriers, cultural, racial and religious, and the difficulties involved in that, gave an illustration of such a 'meal' in his inaugural sermon, which was recounted to me. He works in Sheffield and regularly walks along an underpass. Here a man was sleeping rough. Inderjit one day engaged him in conversation, to find out something of his story. Moved by being noticed and being accepted as worthy of some-one's time, the rough stranger asked the minister whether he would like some bread. Expecting a crust, Inderjit said yes, but instead the old man put out a piece of wood as a table and placed on it a whole range of breads that he had been given from

Marks & Spencer. He offered Inderjit a choice, and then more.
By allowing the man to be himself, Inderjit felt that what he had
discovered was a true Eucharist, a sharing of the broken Body
of Christ, a meal like those New Testament meals. He showed
by his acceptance of the other that 'I am uniquely me, and you
are uniquely you.'

Of course issues involving the homeless are complex, and this
incident touches only one moment in what may be a tragic story.
Nevertheless, through this simple action, in one small way, the
liberation of the other becomes my liberation also. A contrast
has been made between a Western view of freedom, that it
is about 'freedom from others', and an Eastern view, which is
'freedom for others'. Those like this street dweller, excluded by
the norms of society, offer a challenge to us. If we give them the
freedom to be themselves, it can on occasion free us from our
fears and enable us to enrich ourselves and be free for others.

The same can apply within the even more complex world of
those afflicted by HIV/AIDS, where a whole range of fears may
make us seek freedom by separation from them. We pretend the
disease does not exist, or will go away, or is something that
happens in Africa or just to gay men whom we avoid. Recently
I attended a consultation for the annual AIDS day. Stereotypes
were broken down as we met six different people. One was a
gay man, kept alive by drugs, who made us understand how
wretched it was to take the cocktail with all its side effects. A
second was a middle-class woman in her fifties, not the kind of
person one associates with HIV/AIDS. The third was an African
postgraduate student who had decided, with a group of three
friends, to get themselves tested while in this country and anonymous: three of the four were HIV positive. The other three
people were a family – a white man married to a Kenyan woman,
with a two-year-old daughter. The little girl asks frequently why
she has to take so many pills.

Rather than this exposure creating fear, I experienced a sense
of freedom as people listened and related to them, not as a
class of AIDS sufferers, but as people each unique in themselves.
The woman also revealed a sense of liberation as she 'came out'
with us, in a way that she had never done with her own parents,

those who lived down her street or those who were her fellow worshippers on Sunday. Her liberation and our liberation were bound up together.

Moving from the individual to communities and cultures, the challenge is how both to rejoice in our own culture and to allow others to be themselves in their culture. It is also how to enable mutual enrichment, by which we can feel free and unthreatened as we rejoice in what each has to offer, rather than remain entirely in ghetto worlds. Religion has so often been either the destruction of culture or an instrument for raising barriers between cultures. Discussion in contemporary Britain is about how to do this, to be British and also to be affirmed in owning a particular culture, often bound up with religious dimensions. No culture is self-sufficient, unchanging and beyond criticism.

What is needed is a healthy self-criticism, a lack of defensiveness and a willingness to listen to others, who must also be willing themselves to receive such an appraisal. Someone from outside a culture can often see what the person steeped in it cannot see. The outsiders need permission to express their judgement. I had been in India for a year or so, when the principal of the seminary in which I was teaching called me and said, 'Andrew, you have made every effort to learn our language and understand our culture. I am impressed by where you have got to by listening and learning. Now I would like you to speak up about where you feel things may be wrong in the way we do things or decide things. We may not change but would like to hear what you see as an outsider who is alongside us.'

Very different was much of the impact of missions upon indigenous cultures, not just centuries ago but in recent times. The encounters between South American Protestant missionaries and Amerindian cultures were examined a few years ago in a BBC film *The Road to Eldorado*. The missionaries evangelised the local Indian communities who had been cut off from the modern world. Their way of life was very distinctive and self-sustaining. It had what seemed to the outsider harsh and undesirable features. But at the same time it enabled a strong sense of community and mutual support, where 'I' and 'my family' were not dominant, but 'us' and 'our community'. They had their own

legends and myths and a sense of the spiritual, which covered
all aspects of life. The evangelisers were not aggressive people,
they did not rush in, but spent a long time in preparation. But
the compound they set up for Christian converts was one where
a life was established gently to deculturise the converts from
these peoples, to enable them to learn a new way, the way of
Christ, which would remove them from their past. The Christian
Gospel was not one that embraced and baptised what was good
in their culture; it was one that imposed its own South American
Protestant culture. Because the missionaries did not allow the
others freedom to be Christians within their own culture, they
lost the chance to free themselves from some of the destructive
cultural accretions of the 'Protestant culture' inherited from
North America, with its materialism, individualism and success-
orientation.

In Britain, especially in our mainline churches, it has been
difficult for those of minority ethnic background to feel free
to be themselves, to feel they have not just permission but
encouragement to offer from their own riches of experience. This
applies to those of Asian and African backgrounds and it also
affects those from youth cultures or working-class cultures in
primarily middle-aged, elderly or middle-class churches. Here,
the imperative is to free ourselves from our church structures, to
go to where people actually are, to meet them where their need
is, so that they can feel free to express themselves in their own
way. Two passages from a report of which I was one of the
writers, *Good News in Our Times*,[6] explain this:

> How often, if a regular punter at the local pub died, would
> the vicar visit the pub, to say a prayer, to listen to emotions,
> to keep silence with those left behind? In a parish in
> Coventry, the hostility between a local predominantly black
> youth club and the church was felt to disappear overnight
> when the curate chose, on the death of a 19-year-old member
> of the club, to go along on club night and lead five minutes'
> silence and the singing of a couple of hymns.

A youth worker felt the vast gap between the culture of the
church and that of the young people he encountered on the streets.

He organised a gathering and after some time introduced a way of worship which drew on their world:

> Part of the evening was social, when young people could speak about what they wished. During the rest of the evening he enabled them to make their own worship, prayer and sermon. They wrote simple prayers and songs, and drew cartoons, which they explained; the group shared stories, and maybe acted one out. And everything was done in their vocabulary. Only slowly was the Bible introduced. The young people were the creators, and not just the audience.

One of the critical questions in considering any culture from a Christian perspective, including our own, whatever that is, concerns the criteria for affirming aspects of a culture and the criteria for not being able to affirm. Without these, there is a real danger that we affirm only what is consonant with our own cultural values. This is why there are alarm signals when politicians raise questions about the need to integrate with 'British culture' or with 'civilised values'. Whose culture and whose values?

The same report suggests a list of criteria for measuring what is considered authenticity of culture. The belief is that these values, as found in any culture, 'point us to God's continuing work in Jesus Christ', whether that is acknowledged, implicit or unrecognised. I include the list of ten such criteria here because they contain a testimony to the theme of this chapter, that of freeing others to be themselves, and the setting at liberty of those who are oppressed:[7]

> *The recognition that the entire created order is a gift of God* (Ps 24.1; 1 Cor 3.21b-23).
>
> *The affirmation of the supreme values of justice and loving-kindness* (Is 58.6-7; Mt 23.23).
>
> *The acceptance of the fact that all human beings are to be accorded equality in dignity and worth* (Acts 10.34).
>
> *An awareness of the existence of evil and suffering in the world* (Gen 6.13; Heb 2.14-18).
>
> *The experience of forgiveness and reconciliation* (Col 1.21-22; Mt 5.23-24).

The fostering of hope in a transformed order of human life
(1 Peter 1.3).
The entering upon a new way of being human (2.Cor.5.17).
The enjoyment of responsible freedom (Gal 5.13).
The creation of life in community (Rom 12.5).
The celebration of the Good News (Ps 145; Lk 15.22-24).

Each has an explanatory paragraph. To take only *The enjoyment of responsible freedom*, it says:

> This enjoyment is the fruit of liberation *from* the bondage
> of self-centredness and, at the same time, it derives from
> liberation *for* a life of self-giving and the service of others.
> Power can then be exercised not over other people but in
> partnership with them and on their behalf.

This giving of freedom to others to be themselves means freeing
ourselves from the need to dominate, from the illusion that we
offer people a choice, when we really mean 'if you choose what
I want you to choose'. We think that we are free, but in fact such
domination only enslaves the dominator. It can bring an enormous
sense of relief, even liberation, when someone who always takes
decisions directly or indirectly actually allows the other to make
a choice. As this becomes a regular possibility, it is as if a burden
is lifted, that of always having to be at the centre of things.

A particular focus for such experience can be in the area of
forgiveness and reconciliation. When we offer forgiveness and
seek reconciliation and a new start, it can be extremely hurtful
if it is not accepted. A task is to offer what we believe is the
liberating experience of forgiveness. But we cannot force its
acceptance. This can have deep cultural implications, involving
loss of face. It may be that fault is not accepted, and we cannot
force an understanding of it. I remember one of my mature
students of another culture leaving college unreconciled to me.
She felt I had mismanaged, as principal, some issues affecting
her and her community in college life. A third party tried to
reconcile us. He felt he had failed when he could not enable this
to happen. He prayed as we separated, but could find only
stuttering phrases to express what he felt was a failure in relation-

ships. At first I felt upset. But then I let it go; I can only offer reconciliation, the other person is free to reject what I offer.

Another incident involved two students, one white, and one black South African. The white student, a priest, felt deeply hurt that it seemed he was being blamed for all the colonial and apartheid history that had deeply damaged the people represented by the young woman he was trying to share community with. He was particularly hurt that she would not shake hands with him at the eucharistic peace, though he held out his hand. It came to the last days before they were both to leave, she to return to South Africa, he to go to work with the Church in Zimbabwe. He was in anguish: how could he go to Africa, if he was not accepted by an African here? Both parties were unhappy, but not freed to free each other. But on the last night, the Holy Spirit intervened! The woman was finishing her last essay when her computer crashed. The priest was an expert, and no one else was around. She had to turn to him, and he fixed it for her and saved her work. He held out his hand and she took it. At the Eucharist on the final day there was a real peace between them and a sense of liberation as they each allowed the other to be themselves, but within a mutual acceptance in Christ.

Political dimensions can run very deep. Christian freedom calls for the emancipation of the oppressed. Through such emancipation comes also the freeing of the oppressor, but only if the oppression is willingly lifted. If there is no intention to free the oppressed, the oppressor remains enchained in a prison of their own, or of historical, making. To take two examples – debt and racism – the present world may not be directly responsible for the terms of trade and neo-colonial conditions that have led to the realities of international debt. The liberation of deeply indebted countries is a matter of justice and restitution. But through the remission of such debts, there will come the liberation of the oppressors from a system which in the end will bring the world, including themselves, to self-destruction. Racism clearly has its victims, who need liberation from the consequences of racist attitudes and actions. But that liberation alone can also enable the oppressor to be freed from racist attitudes, conscious or unconscious, which enslave and prevent openness to the other. Such freedom is primary.

As Christians we may know the truth of these sentiments, but feel that there is nothing we can do as individuals to change our world and its systems, powerless as we are. These two examples suggest otherwise. Trevor Huddleston, an Anglican priest from Britain, worked in Sophiatown, Johannesburg, in the 1950s. The rapidly developing apartheid system of social segregation seemed to him deeply anti-Christian, leading to the enslavement not just of the blacks, but of the whites who were imposing the system. He wrote *Naught for Your Comfort* in 1956, as an alarm cry to South Africa, and to the wider world. Opposed by the Church establishment in both South Africa and Britain, he faced withdrawal from South Africa by his own religious Order with sadness but conviction that theology and justice would win in the end. He wrote later that he and one or two other clergy spoke up, but the laity sat in their pews with their hands firmly on their knees. He saw the solution to South Africa's problems as simple: 'It lies in the simple recognition that ALL men are made in "the image and likeness of God": that in consequence each PERSON is of infinite and eternal value: that the State exists to protect the person but is in itself always of inferior value to the person.'

He was to return to South Africa 40 years later to a liberated country, which still had deep inherited problems, but with his stand on freedom and worth vindicated. On the way, the liberation of Nelson Mandela, so esteemed by Huddleston, became the means of liberating so many of his enemies. On a lesser scale, but no less real for that, we see the brave steps being taken by the parents of Stephen Lawrence, the black teenager brutally murdered in London, to highlight the fight against the racism that had killed their son and that enchains many in modern Britain. Out of a Christian conviction for justice, they spearhead a fight to free others from the enslavement of racism, both oppressed and oppressors.

Another individual is Bill Peters. A retired diplomat, he could have been excused if he had concentrated on having a peaceful life supporting his local church. But the situation of countries in which he had served now being enslaved by crippling and life-denying debt played on his mind. Eventually, with a fellow retired person, an academic, he began what became the Jubilee 2000 campaign. From small beginnings early in the 1990s, it became an internationally known and respected movement that could confront governments and G7 summits. It has not achieved all that it set out to complete, but it has focused many minds, and led to major steps in the right direction. The message has been that freedom is indivisible, that my freeing you from your debt also frees me from the consequences of that debt. To achieve what has been achieved has required enormous tenacity, not least from Bill Peters, who was prepared to irritate on every occasion to make sure the case was heard. Because of Jubilee 2000 many Africans' lives have been tangibly improved and, perhaps more important, there is a new mindset worldwide on questions of the inequity of international debt.

It has been said that the person who feels they can do nothing has ceased to be a Christian. These two individuals and many like them represent a special call to do something about the liberation of others, something central to the Christian Gospel.

A prayer that sums up this invitation to be free, and to allow others to be free, is called 'Touch Me with Truth that Burns like Fire' (author unknown):

> Lord, send the gift of your Spirit to fill this place and
>   myself and the world.
> Touch me with truth that burns like fire, with beauty that
>   moves me like the wind;
> And set me free, Lord.
> Free to try new ways of living, free to forgive myself and
>   others,
> Free to love and laugh and sing,
> Free to lay aside my burden of security,
> Free to join the battle for justice and peace,
> Free to see and listen and wonder again
> At the gracious mystery of things and persons;
> Free to be, to give, to receive, to rejoice as a child of your
>   Spirit.
> And, Lord, teach me how to dance,

To turn around and come down where I want to be,
In the arms and hearts of your people, and in you,
That I may praise and enjoy you forever.

Readers' response

- Who in your life do you try to control, to make conform to
  what you would have them be? How specifically could you
  take steps to free them to be themselves? How would you feel
  if they took those steps?

- Consider the community of your local congregation. Are
  people allowed to be themselves and to offer their gifts? How
  could you encourage one particular person to be more themselves and offer what they have to the congregation or the
  wider community?

- In your local context, name someone who has taken clear steps
  to bring freedom from oppression to a particular group of
  people. Is there anything you could do to help that person and
  their movement?

Passages for meditation

Henri Nouwen, *Bread for the Journey*, p.34:

To forgive another person from the heart is an act of
liberation. We set that person free from the negative
bonds that exist between us. We say, 'I no longer hold
your offence against you'. But there is more. We also free
ourselves from the burden of being the 'offended one'.
As long as we do not forgive those who have wounded
us, we carry them with us or, worse, pull them as a heavy
load. The great temptation is to cling in anger to our
enemies and then define ourselves as being offended and
wounded by them. Forgiveness therefore liberates not
only the other but also ourselves. It is the way to the
freedom of the children of God.

Bread for the Journey, p.83:

We spend an enormous amount of energy making up our minds about other people. Not a day goes by without somebody doing or saying something that evokes in us the need to form an opinion about him or her. We hear a lot, see a lot and know a lot. The feeling that we have to sort it all out in our minds and make judgements about it can be quite oppressive.

The desert fathers said that judging others is a heavy burden, while being judged by others is a light one. Once we can let go of our need to judge others, we will experience an immense inner freedom. Once we are free from judging, we will be also free for mercy. Let's remember Jesus' words, 'Do not judge, and you will not be judged.' (Matthew 7:1).

Dietrich Bonhoeffer, *Life Together*, pp.70–1:

It must be a decisive rule of every Christian fellowship that each individual is prohibited from saying much that occurs to him. Where this discipline of the tongue is practised right from the beginning, each individual will make a matchless discovery. He will be able to cease from constantly scrutinizing the other person, judging him, condemning him, putting him in his particular place where he can gain ascendancy over him and thus doing violence to him as a person.

Now he can allow the brother to exist as a completely free person, as God made him to be. Now the other person, in the freedom with which he was created, becomes the occasion of joy, whereas before he was only a nuisance and an affliction.

Life Together, pp.77–8:

The law of Christ is a law of bearing. Bearing means forbearing and sustaining. The Christian must bear the burden of a brother. He must suffer and endure the brother.

It is, first of all, the freedom of the other person, of

which we spoke earlier, that is a burden to the Christian. The other's freedom collides with his own autonomy, yet he must recognise it. He could get rid of this burden by refusing the other person his freedom, by constraining him and thus doing violence to his personality, by stamping his own image upon him. But if he lets God create his image in him, he by this token gives him his freedom and himself bears the burden of this freedom of another creature of God.

The freedom of the other person includes all that we mean by a person's nature, individuality, endowment. It also includes his weaknesses and oddities, which are such a trial to our patience, everything that produces frictions, conflicts and collisions among us.

Chapter 5

FREEDOM AND CONVERSION

Genesis 12:1–9; Matthew 19:16–22

Then the Lord said to Abram, 'Go from your country and your kindred and your father's house to the land that I will show you. I will make of you a great nation, and I will bless you, and make your name great, so that you will be a blessing.'

Genesis 12:1–2

Jesus said to him, 'If you wish to be perfect, go, sell your possessions, and give the money to the poor, and you will have treasure in heaven; then come and follow me.' When the young man heard this word, he went away grieving, for he had many possessions.

Matthew 19:21–2

Omar has been granted political asylum in Leicester. He feels a strong sense of liberation from the oppression he felt in the Middle Eastern country that he still loves deeply. He left because he had attended some Christian meetings, been reported to the police, tortured and dismissed from his professional training. His father had been very angry, and his mother had provided the money – he comes from a wealthy family – to travel concealed on a lorry to Europe. The journey of eight days was a nightmare. He had no idea where he was or where he was going until he arrived in Dover. No sooner had he got over this journey than he was 'dispersed' two hundred miles away to Leicester. Here his safe haven was a large 'hotel' where up to four hundred single persons are housed at a time, often two or three to a room. It is not a prison, but sometimes seems like one because of its rules and its pervasive sense of institutionalisation. Here he stayed for more than a year, until his appeal was finally upheld, with a little help from two of us who could speak for him and be his advocates.

Omar came to Leicester as a searcher. He had endured all this suffering because he was not happy with the version of Islam that he had experienced. He was willing to undergo all this privation because of his longing for a new start. In Leicester he attended a Baptist church from the first Sunday after he arrived. Struggling with rudimentary English, which improved week by week, he found out more of the Christian faith. Eventually he decided to seek baptism. Long preparation followed, and his baptism happened only after he had been given asylum. At a moving service of baptism by immersion, before a large congregation he gave a testimony, where somehow he was able to transcend his linguistic difficulties. I was reminded of the way St Paul describes how the Spirit comes to the aid of our weakness and gives us words when we do not know how to find them. The key concept in the witness he made was that he felt 'free', 'liberated'. He had found 'life'. Important too had been the tangible sense of 'fellowship' he had received within the congregation. He had given up family, country, home, car, good prospects, for deprivation, humiliation and an unknown future where his practical problems are only just beginning. Yet what he was experiencing was 'freedom'. For him 'freedom' and 'conversion' are inextricably linked together.

In this chapter I will be considering this aspect of freedom. Inter-religious conversion does not happen just towards Christianity; we need to consider this as an aspect of freedom that can work in the direction of other religions also. The word can also be used within a religion, as part of a lifelong process, or as a result of a specific experience.

Conversion, of course, does not necessarily mean 'liberation' or 'freedom'. Some movements to which people turn are far from liberating, and the word 'enslaving' would be a better description. Additionally, some people, whether consciously or subconsciously, do not seek freedom through submitting themselves to a new idea or religion. Rather they are seeking, at best, order and discipline, at worst an authority figure or organisation which will deprive them of the possibility of thinking for themselves and enable them to replace the fear of freedom with the simplicity of obedience. Such persons choose to change their faith and way of life deliberately to avoid the risk of freedom and what they find as anarchy in the modern world, where they suffer from a kind of existential angst, that they are, in a popular phrase 'alone and afraid in a world they never made'. They freely accept a conversion which involves the suppression of desire and even skills and inner gifts. Those who know them well see them becoming a pale shadow of what they were. Far from appearing to be liberated, they seem imprisoned, even though they may use the rhetoric of freedom.

I was once involved in counselling a woman who felt that her marriage was in great danger of breaking up because of her husband's conversion to a pseudo-Christian sect. He had become two personalities: the one she knew, loved and had married, and was still partly there, and the one he became when he had been to meetings of the sect. There he lost himself in something that she experienced as enslaving and evil. She came to me because he had told her that, unless she followed him into the sect, he would be pressurised to divorce her and make a new beginning. This she did not want to happen, but there was no way she was willing to join him in what she experienced through him as imprisonment.

Another example is a highly intelligent Cambridge student who came under the influence of what she described as a 'new age' sect. She married someone who had become a devotee. They took up quite innocent and indeed beneficial things such as vegetarianism, meditation and various worthy causes. At the same time, they were introduced to much more questionable activities, including what felt like occult practices. Before it was too late, she stepped back, realising that her freedom was disappearing inch by inch. She was losing her life, not into the freedom of something greater, but into something dark and restrictive.

We need to be clear, therefore, that not all conversion relates to liberation. This is obviously so where the kind of movements mentioned above are concerned, but it applies also within 'mainline' religions. As is well known, converts are often more zealous and with their zeal can come a deep intolerance. They have given their life to what is new, and it almost seems as if to show any doubts or hesitations is to deny what they may have suffered greatly for. This is particularly so when there is real hate for their former faith, and they show no grace or freedom in acknowledging what it had given to them, at least by way of preparation for a change.

An example is a Brahmin Hindu who drifted away from his family and faith while at university. He took to drink and a wild life, and began to despise what he now called idol worship amongst his family. In despair, he took an overdose, and was rehabilitated by Christian friends. He eventually came to baptism, feeling at peace and liberated from his lostness. He became evangelical in commending his new faith. At the same time, he became deeply hostile to the faithful Hindus who had brought him up and taught him of God. There seemed little love at the centre of a person who was now so sure that he was right and superior. As I talked with him, I found it hard to use the word 'liberation'.

Another ambiguous aspect of conversion is its relationship to culture. Though there are some sides of culture to be freed from which may appear a blessing, there are also experiences of deculturisation which seem entirely negative. In terms of Christianity, this is a struggle for most non-Western converts, particularly those from societies where religion and culture are highly intertwined. One high-caste Hindu convert told me that he felt he had to become a 'coconut' – brown on the outside, white within – in order to conform to the norms expected in his Anglican church. Another felt that he had to conceal his identity when returning on visits to India. No one would worry about his conversion to Jesus Christ, their problem would be about his 'sell-out' to Westernisation and the church. A survey in 1992 showed that more than two thirds of Hindus who enter churches and can be counted as 'converts' to Christianity in Britain revert within a year. The reason is not a failure of faith, an unwillingness to follow Jesus as their liberating Lord, but a cultural and social one, preventing them feeling at home in their new context. They cannot be themselves, they do not feel 'free'.

A classic story about loss of freedom is that of Lispeth. She is the centre of a tale of that name written, perhaps surprisingly, by Rudyard Kipling at the end of the nineteenth century. Lispeth lived in the Himalayan foothills and was a tribal girl. Her parents died from cholera and she was given a home by the wife of the chaplain of the local hill station. She became 'half-servant' and 'half-companion'. She was baptised and named Elizabeth, which the tribal people could only pronounce as 'Lispeth'. She grew up looking beautiful, in spite of the mission station clothes she was forced to wear. She was happy enough and taught in the Sunday school, though her own people hated her because 'she had become a white woman and washed daily'. She loved walking in the local hills, where she felt a sense of freedom.

One day she returned with a young Englishman whom she had found injured and needing help. To the horror of her adopted 'parents' she said this was the man she wished to marry. As he recovered, she went for daily walks with him and was very happy. When he left, not wanting to disturb her, he promised that he loved her and would come back to marry her after he had revisited England. She had no idea where England was, and waited and waited, going each day up into the hills to look for his coming. After three months, the chaplain's wife told her the truth, that the man had no intention of returning, and that she could never marry someone of such 'superior clay'. She explained, to Lispeth's disbelief, that the promise had been an excuse to keep her quiet. Lispeth left her adopted home forthwith, saying their lies had killed Lispeth. She returned to her own people, the dress of a hill girl and to her tribal gods. Her beauty faded quickly in the rough life to which she returned, and especially after she married a woodcutter, who beat her.

The chaplain's wife reflected, 'I believe that Lispeth was always at heart an infidel.'

Lispeth's conversion was never a liberation, nor was her reversion a liberation either. She was condemned forever to live in a kind of limbo. Kipling affixes this short poem:

> Look, you have cast out Love! What Gods are these you
>   bid me please?
> The Three in One, the One in Three? Not so! To my own
>   gods I go.
> It may be that they shall give me greater ease than your
>   cold Christ and tangled Trinities.

It is a poignant story which raises in extreme fashion the disastrous consequences of a conversion which is enslaving and not liberating. Lispeth had been totally deculturised, as she was 'born again' in a Christian household. She lost her name, her language and her way of dressing. She was not unhappy in her new state, but something inside her kept her in the hills, in spite of the rejection she received from her own community. They confused that fact that she had become Christian with becoming a white woman. The love affair and the lies that followed brought deep disillusionment, not only about the persons concerned but also about their religion. Reversion was easy, and the Christians found it easier to blame her for backsliding than themselves for the way they had treated her. The poem attached to the story points the same lesson in theological terms: that love is more important than doctrine to the convert. For love is liberating, doctrine can be stifling.

Group conversion is another story. Most converts in South Asia and Africa have converted in families, villages or groups. This usually happens for a combination of reasons, but in the Indian context, liberation from oppression, usually caste oppression, is often a central factor. The village of Veerambal is in one of the poorest areas of Tamilnadu. Its Dalit community were living in bonded labour to higher caste landlords who owned all the land. They were treated as slaves, and their women often used as such sexually. In the 1950s they heard the Gospel. They heard of a Jesus Christ who loved untouchables and set them free, and that in the Church which he inspired 'there is to be no Jew nor Greek, no male nor female, no slave nor free'. For them this meant 'no high caste or low caste or Dalit'. They took baptism together and built a church. The landlords did not like this, and even less so when the converts demanded time off on a Sunday morning to worship. Sunday became a symbol for their true liberation, very much on the lines of one of the Old Testament understandings of Sabbath. In Deuteronomy 5, Moses prefaces the reading of the Ten Commandments with verse 6: 'I am the Lord your God who brought you out of the land of Egypt, out of the house of slavery.' To observe Sunday and to come out of bonded labour to offer their services for a free wage were essential corollaries to their religious conversion.

A battle ensued and three members of the new Christian community were killed. Their descendants today will show the visitor bullet holes in the church walls, a memorial to what they see as their 'exodus' struggle. Eventually, with the assistance of their bishop, Lesslie Newbigin, the Dalits won their freedom. They have had many struggles since, and in the new India it is in their interests to revert to Hinduism, since only as Hindus will they get the full help available to Dalits. But they are quite clear that they have made their choice for freedom. Along with this has gone a sense of dignity and self-respect, and educational attainment as they have taken advantage of Christian schools. For them conversion has meant liberation and freedom.

For others it has not been such a happy story. I researched two villages which had been converted to Christianity in earlier days, for reasons similar to Veerambal. But their experience in the church is that though they gained education, they did not gain acceptance as Dalits. They remained on the outside. Sometimes this was literal. I met a higher-caste Christian who said that she was happy to visit them to pray and mix with them in church. But she must not expect them to enter her house, or that she should eat with them, let alone marry her children to them. She agreed that these attitudes did not match those of Jesus in the gospels, but he had no weddings to arrange!

It is not surprising that when an Islamic mission visited the village they had considerable success, not just with Hindus, but also with Christians. Their message was clear, that in Islam there was equality and liberation from untouchability. There was also a freedom from complicated doctrines such as the Trinity. This they demonstrated in an admission ceremony which I witnessed. Existing Muslims embraced new Muslims as part of this ceremony. Food was then shared from a common pot, and each person eating had to take a handful of rice from their own plate and place it on the plate of their neighbour. This was a very powerful demonstration of how untouchability was being removed at a stroke. Conversion was experienced as liberation.

A difficult challenge is raised here. If we hold an inclusive understanding of God, that God has not left himself without a witness in any community or culture and that the Spirit can be active outside the Church, how do we see a story like this? The Church at its best reveals a God of love, righteousness, liberation, freedom and salvation. That is why – above all, I would argue – groups and individuals convert to membership. But if such converts gradually become aware that they have not found such realities within the Church, and that the gap between the Gospel heard and the Church experienced is too great, could it be that the God in Christ to whom they converted might be better experienced outside the mainline churches? This might be within fellowships explicitly acknowledging Christ. But could God on occasions even lead them beyond the Christian fold to another religion, such as Islam or Buddhism or some forms of Hinduism? Perhaps it might be that God in Christ meets them there on the way, at least for a time, as they experience something more liberating.

This challenge has also been raised for me by individuals in Britain. An intelligent Scottish woman who has converted to Islam wears Islamic dress and plays a full part in her new faith. The stereotype I hear so often expressed is that Islam is a mechanical religion, and that women are oppressed within it. This woman is a living witness against such thinking. She is articulate and clear about why she is glad to be a Muslim. There is no sense of oppression. Above all she talks of how she has left no God behind, the Church of Scotland God and Allah are the same. But she now feels liberated because she no longer has the hierarchy of the Church to suffer. She also has a personal relationship with God, which makes her free. It is not easy for Christians to hear, but this is her testimony. Another woman Muslim convert spoke of how through Islam she has a direct relationship with God. She feels free because she no longer has to go through a mediator.

Such a challenge has also been raised by certain converts to Buddhism. There are now quite a large number of converts of European origin in Britain. Some have found themselves liberated from depression, disillusion, perhaps drugs or alcohol. Very different is a Buddhist friend who had been brought up in a strong Roman Catholic family. Conversion came, as so often happens, in her student years, and again, not unusually, by a series of seemingly random incidents. She already felt pushed away from her family faith, which she experienced as restricting. Buddhism happened to come to her notice. She has a philosophical mind and was led into the depths of its philosophy. She became a Tibetan Buddhist and began to share her new faith with Western groups. She became deeply involved in the interfaith movement and taught Buddhist–Christian dialogue with me. In the 15 years I have known her, I have seen her both deepening her conversion to Buddhism, and at the same time relating more affectionately and positively to the Christianity in which she had been brought up, meeting it again as though it were a new thing. Through the openness of her belief in Buddhism she has become free to relate anew to her past.

Another example is from Sikhism. A *gurdwara* in Birmingham has a number of 'monks'. One is European. He is a young man who lives in the *gurdwara* all the time, wearing the same simple white cotton clothes as his Punjabi colleagues. Whilst his peer group spend their lives furthering their careers, and in their leisure visiting public houses, watching television and seeking girlfriends, he spends two hours a day in the morning, and up to four hours in the evening, in devotion. In between he studies the Sikh religion and learns Punjabi. He is now able to read the scriptures to the congregation of two hundred who meet there each evening. I experience him as at peace with the enormous step he has taken, in face of almost total unbelief from his nominally Christian family. Though he has taken vows which mean he will never leave the *gurdwara*, he seems a free person.

Such a link between conversion and liberation is found, of course, amongst those who have converted to Christ as well. Apart from Omar mentioned at the start of this chapter, I write here of three examples from Britain who will stand for the many I have known and whose stories I have researched, in India and in Britain.

The first is a woman in her twenties, of Hindu background and from a large family. As a younger daughter, she found little affirmation there and used to long to go out, which she was allowed to do only by going to work. She was depressed and identified only loosely with her religion. Each day she passed a church. One day, courageously, she went in and sat and looked at the beautiful stained glass windows, which told the story of Jesus. On another day she took this further and went to sit in a lunchtime service called 'Holy Eucharist'. Afterwards a woman priest explained things to her. They became friends and gradually the girl learned of the Christian religion. She read the Bible secretly, and eventually, after some months, freely decided to become a disciple of Jesus Christ. She felt a deep peace, now feeling fully loved by God.

Some time later, she took courage into her hands and told her parents. They were predictably negative, reflecting on what they had done wrong that this terrible thing should come upon them. She, however, has remained firm, and their psychological pressure has failed to make her turn back on her free decision. As I talked with her, I often felt a sense of 'awe' at the journey she has taken, and the way she can articulate this. She talks freely with me, despite all my academic degrees, as an equal, and her knowledge of scripture is quite remarkable. She quotes, for example, Psalm 27:10, 'If my father and my mother forsake me, the Lord will take me up.' Her struggles have continued before and after baptism, but I have no doubt that the words 'conversion' and 'freedom' go together in her story. Her determination has also won her much more freedom of movement, as well as the freedom of her inner spirit.

The second example is Iyengar. He is unusual as a Brahmin convert to Christianity. He was born in Madras but brought up in London, where his father was a trustee of the local temple. As a young man he put on the sacred thread. He went to Roman Catholic schools, where he learned of Christianity and acted in nativity plays. It was a positive experience that he took away with him to university. There he encountered Christians and was impressed by them, though not at first by the church. Eventually, much to the anger and sadness of his parents he took baptism. His brother said, 'You have become a *shudra* [low-caste man] now.'

Iyengar married an Irish woman, and at their wedding he asked the priest to preach on the text 'Perfect love casts out all fear.' For him, 'God is love' is the most important message of Christianity, and one that liberates from all caste and ritual fears. Also he feels freed from karma and its consequences by the liberating death of Jesus Christ, when forgiveness is offered to all. He still had some way to go in liberating himself from his Brahmin superiority, he realised, when on a return visit to Madras, he was receiving change from a woman in a newspaper kiosk. He cupped his hands for her to put the money into. She said, 'This is remarkable. You have been in London so long and yet you still know I should not touch you.' This hurt him; as a Christian he should have been able to let her touch him.

He has struggled also to free himself from an over-Westernised Christianity that he converted into, and from a narrowness of theology. An old Hindu friend of his died, and Iyengar wrote to me: 'I cannot believe my old Hindu friend will not be accepted by the love of God. The fruit of the Spirit was so evident in him. Often it appears that people are not led by missionaries to understand Christ as the fulfilment of their quest, but that their very quest is demolished.' He reveals here a maturity that is struggling with real questions. He is also concerned about the position of his parents before God, those who taught him about God. He longs to be freed from the kind of rigid exclusivism that would confine them to hell. At the same time an easy universalism would seem to deny the kind of journey that he has made, which he feels has been a journey towards personal freedom.

My last example is Ismet, a young Muslim woman from a doctor's family. Her mother was an Asian Christian, but her father brought the children up very strictly as Muslims, often the way in mixed marriages. She was even given a bicycle for memorising the whole of the Qur'an. He forbade their mother to take them to church, but this she did when he was away. The home became very tense and this was linked for Ismet with a real fear of Islam, with her father's insistent demand for obedience in the name of Allah. She moved towards Christianity and eventually told her father, who said that she was no longer his daughter and that she would go to hell. He even used occult practices against her and her mother. Inevitably a divorce followed for her mother.

At last Ismet felt free to be open in her faith. She was now able to attend church as she wished, and it was a place of warmth and community in her troubled life. She felt that the Holy Spirit had been working in her life, and she had experienced this as the spirit of liberation. She became a social worker and married another convert, this time from Hinduism, who had also suffered for his faith journey. Together they feel free to face the world.

There can also, of course, be conversion to and from atheism. C. S. Lewis is the most famous example of a convert from atheism in recent times, with his journey recorded in his book *Surprised by Joy*. In a rather different vein are the meditations in *Markings*, written by the former General Secretary of the United Nations Dag Hammarskjöld, killed in an air crash in the Congo in 1961. It is the spiritual diary of a private man. One of the last entries records what was to prove to be his final testimony, and it is a testimony to freedom:[1]

> I don't know Who – or what – put the question, I don't know when it was put. I don't even remember answering. But at some moment I did answer *Yes*, to Someone – or Something – and from that hour I was certain that existence is meaningful and that, therefore, my life, in self-surrender,

had a goal. From that moment I have known what it means 'not to look back', and 'to take no thought for the morrow'.

. . . As I continued along the Way, I learned, step by step, word by word, that behind every saying in the Gospels, stands *one* man and *one* man's experience. Also behind the prayer that the cup might pass from him and his promise to drink it. And behind each of the words from the Cross.

Conversely, here are examples of two contemporary Anglican priests who found themselves converted, away from what they had found increasingly was living a lie. Professor Michael Goulder of Birmingham University continued as an eminent biblical scholar and teacher, but found himself released from a great burden when he became honest with himself and declared himself an atheist. More recent has been the testimony of Anthony Freeman, a priest in Chichester Diocese, who found he no longer believed what he was preaching and teaching. Though not naming himself an atheist, but seeing God in non-realist terms, he wrote down his position in a popular book, for which he was dismissed from his post. Again he appeared to find a great sense of liberation.

How is conversion to be defined, and how do such definitions relate to our theme of freedom? The classic psychologist's definition is that of William James, who wrote:[2]

> To be converted, to be regenerated, to experience religion, to gain an assurance, are so many phrases which denote the process, gradual or sudden, by which a self, hitherto divided and consciously wrong, inferior or unhappy, becomes unified and consciously right, superior and happy in consequence of its firmer hold upon religious realities.

This definition fits the classical stories of conversion, such as those of Augustine, John Wesley, Martin Luther and John Henry Newman. A sense of alienation, disarray or guilt is through conversion replaced by a sense of freedom, integration and hope. Martin Luther was thoroughly disturbed by the state of the church in which he served as a monk. It appears to have been making him physically ill. Then one day in 1517, he suddenly realised

the truth of Romans 1:16–17, that 'The one who is righteous
will live by faith.' Faith was the free gift of grace. He no longer
had to struggle with his conscience, and could feel happy and
right with God. Similarly with St Augustine, as he came to terms
with his struggle over guilt about past sins, from stealing apples
to sexual misdemeanours. Liberated by conversion to his doctrine
of justification by faith through grace, he was at peace with
himself and God. As he indicates in his famous prayer, his heart,
which had been restless, could at last find its rest with God. For
this kind of conversion, the word 'liberation' is very appropriate.
The Prodigal Son is its paradigm, and it is echoed in the conversion hymn of John Newton, 'Amazing Grace . . . I once was
lost and now am found, was blind and now I see.'

James' definition refers only to a limited number of conver-
sions, individual in character. I also find the word 'superior' in
the definition difficult, with all the dangers of religious arrogance.
The twentieth century bore terrible consequences from this view.

Very different is the definition of Mahatma Gandhi. Conversion is 'self-purification and self-realisation'. As a typical Hindu,
Gandhi does not believe in conversion that leads people to cross
religious frontiers. The task is that of daily conversion within the
religion into which one is born, to find liberation and salvation
there. This means freeing oneself from what is earthly and con-
tingent, to discover one's true self and unity with God. He comments: 'I know that God will ask and asks us now, not what we
label ourselves, but what we are, i.e. what we do. With Him deed
is everything, belief without doing is not believing.'

Such a definition fits well with much Buddhist thought. It also
has an appeal to many Westerners. It is about a journey of self-
discovery and personal growth. For Gandhi this always took place
in relation to society, hence the emphasis on deeds. For him, to
engage in politics and action for justice was a way of self-
realisation, so also to practise *ahimsa*, the way of non-violent
struggle.

The Roman Catholic theologian Karl Rahner defines conversion as 'a fundamental decision not wholly accessible to analytical reflection. Every conversion is only a beginning, and the
rest of it daily fidelity; the conversion which can only be carried

out in a whole lifetime has still to come.'[3] Rahner emphasises the depth of what happens in conversion both by using the word 'fundamental' and by recognising that the moment of adherence to the new faith means little without what follows, which takes a whole lifetime. The conversion story is never finished. An adult baptism is an outward sign of a period of preparation and decision-making. If it is not followed up, and there is no daily practice of faith, attending Mass and commitment to kingdom values, then it is hard to say that conversion has really happened at all. Freedom has to be worked for continually, or reversion takes place.

Rahner may appear to be taking an easy way out with his phrase 'not wholly accessible to analytical reflection'. There are clearly psychological, theological, sociological and other tools available to engage in such an analysis. But in the end we are dealing with the deepest things of the heart and the soul, and are immersed in the mystery of the human person and God's dealing with that person. We can go so far and no further in explaining why a person makes a particular choice. Another person, under the same circumstances and with many of the same characteristics, does not make that choice. Why? Here is a mystery, and we can thank God indeed that each person is unique. We are not machines programmed like computers to act, think, feel or believe in predetermined ways. Recent DNA research shows that each of us has identical genes for the most part. But we each become unique because of the tiny proportion of our genes that are different one from another. We can give thanks for those minority genes. They allow for the variety of human-kind. God alone knows why some make the choice towards liberation, while others prefer to remain where they are.

K. F. Morrison, in his book *Understanding Conversion*, suggests two meanings:[4]

A person embracing a creed, and submitting to an institution that teaches the creed, passes through thick and thin, living out the consequences of acceptance and submission.

A process of redemption that is initiated, sustained or

completed, if at all, by God's action. This involves empathy
and identification with all fellow believers.

Here he distinguishes between, he says, the outward and the
inward, as the difference between those who sing Mozart's Coron-
ation Mass as non-believers and those who believe. Academics
prefer the former, it is more 'objective'. This echoes an illustration from the Danish theologian Søren Kierkegaard. He tells
of people who go into a hall where there are two doors. The first
says 'conversion', and the other 'lecture about conversion'.
People rush for the second door.

Morrison reflects that in the second sense conversion is about
a long haul. Many fall away and the journey is not about self-
fulfilment so much as self-emptying. For Paul it is the crown of
martyrdom that is the reward for such endurance.

The two languages of discourse need to be held together. If
someone claims 'to be freed in Christ' and we see no outward
change in how they behave, and the impression they give is one
of depression rather than of joy or self-confidence, then we may
wonder what is the tangible nature of this 'redemption', this
freeing, at least on this side of death. On the other hand to ignore
the personal testimony to inward experience in the search for a
mirage of objectivity is to see only half the picture. Morrison
writes evocatively in these terms: 'The single word conversion
can have as many layers of meaning as a pearl, and, like a
pearl, can owe its beauty to an original irritant, still to be found
when the process is over, at its core.'

My own definition, based on a large amount of case-study
work in India and Britain is as follows:

> Conversion is a process, including a personal decision, taken
> alone or as part of a group, to centre one's religious life on
> a new focus, which one believes is more liberating, in every
> aspect of that word, and closer to truth. This involves a
> change of identification within oneself, and, normally, a
> change in outward affiliation to a new community, which
> will affect one's life at various levels, 'body, heart, mind
> and soul', and tangible changes of behaviour and religious
> practice.[5]

Here, 'liberation' is a key word, since where this is not experienced, conversion remains fragile at best. And true liberation or freedom cannot be based on what is perceived as falsehood, or less than truth. It is based on integrity and truth, where what is proclaimed and what is lived has a consistency.

I do not here use the term 'Holy Spirit' because it is a definition intended to be inclusive of all inter-religious conversion. But if, like Morrison, I am to reflect from my Christian perspective, I would include that understanding of God as central. It is the Spirit who enables the inclusiveness of the unpredictable in people's lives, and that includes conversion. God is present in and beyond whatever can be imagined in the mystery of the human heart. The Spirit blows where the Spirit wills. The Spirit moved over the waters at creation and it was through the Spirit that God encountered Israel's religious leaders and prophets. In the Wisdom literature, the Spirit is seen as being at the side of God in all God's activity. In the New Testament, the Spirit is seen characterised as the Spirit of Jesus, in the fourth gospel as the *paraclete* who is the comforter, sustainer, advocate, who leads into all truth. In Galatians, the fruits of the Spirit are detailed as love, joy, peace, patience, kindness, goodness, faithfulness and self-control (5:22–3). Where such a Spirit is found, there will be found conversion and liberation.

John Taylor, in his great book on the Spirit, based largely on his experience of God in Africa, wrote these two illuminating passages:[6]

> We have already seen that the most characteristic forms of the action of the Spirit as Creator Redeemer are a constant pressure towards greater personhood, the creation of new occasions for choice, and the principal of self-surrender in responsibility for others. These must be the marks of any evangelism which is truly Christ's evangelism. It must be deeply personal rather than propositional. We have already seen that the truth which converts is the truth *of* Jesus, not the truth *about* Jesus. How strange it is that people who have met the Truth should imagine that they are called to propound truths! How unlike Jesus himself, who would

never violate the freedom and responsibility even of his enemies, are those who would win the world with a loud-hailer in one hand and a book of church statistics in the other.

... [Or, more simply] The evangelism of the Holy Spirit consists in creating the occasions for choice. The servant of the Gospel can do no more, and perhaps need do no more.

The task of Christian mission is not therefore to make converts. Only God can do that. Rather it is to introduce people to choice, to offer them occasions for liberation and life.

If we look at the two biblical passages mentioned at the beginning of the chapter, there is a sharp contrast between the two. Abram was challenged to leave the safety and security of his home country to go out into the desert. His only future security was to rest upon God's promise. This was both that he would be blessed, and that this blessing would be offered through Abram to all the peoples on earth. He was to be an instrument of their liberation, and first he had to make his own choice to go out into the Negev. Because he said yes, he became the first missionary.

He freed himself from his own security, to obey God's call; as Dag Hammarskjöld would have put it, to say 'Yes to Someone – or Something'. Abraham's story in Genesis would also fit another paragraph from the same author:[7]

Led by Ariadne's thread of my answer through the labyrinth of Life, I came to a time and place where I realised that the Way leads to a triumph which is a catastrophe, and to a catastrophe which is a triumph, that the price for committing one's life would be reproach, and that the only elevation possible to man lies in the depths of humiliation. And that the word 'courage' lost its meaning, since nothing could be taken away from me.

No wonder Abraham has become a figure of faith for three religions – Judaism, Christianity and Islam.

The Nobel Peace prizewinner and Jewish writer Elie Wiesel, known for his writing based on the Holocaust experience and especially his novel *Night,* was asked to speak about 'The

Meaning of Freedom' to four thousand US military cadets at West Point. He turned to his Jewish theology, and to Abraham:[8]

> Man is free, for God wants him to be free. All things are foreseen by God, we are told by our Masters, and yet we are free, free to choose every moment of our life. We are free to choose between life and death, between the next instant and death, between good and evil, laughter and tears, free to choose compassion over cruelty, memory over oblivion, beauty over ugliness, morality over immorality, and we are free to choose between freedom and absence of freedom.
>
> ... Though chosen by God to be the first believer, Abraham was free to reject that mission. He could have said no, but he didn't. Does it seem like a paradox? I am free not to be afraid of paradoxes.
>
> The idea, I believe, is simply not to confuse divine freedom and human freedom. The two are connected but not identical. God is free, and man must be free ... Now what is freedom? Freedom to the slave is not the same as freedom to the owner of the slave ... Freedom is not a given: it is something one must constantly fight for. Freedom is not even given by God. Freedom belongs to the human domain. It is up to us to shape and nourish it.

In contrast, the rich young man has become an example of someone who is offered a choice and refuses it. He refuses the choice of freedom, and prefers slavery. He is enchained by his riches, from which he is not able to liberate himself. So he loses the chance of life, of conversion, of freedom. But things may be a little more complicated than that, as we can see from the passage from Bonhoeffer at the end of this chapter.

I will end with a quotation from Alan Ecclestone, the great parish priest and writer I mentioned in an earlier chapter, who died a few years ago, and who lived a life and ministry of risk as he identified always with the concerns of the people in his parishes, most of them poor. He wrote of freedom:[9]

> Freedom means the ability and willingness to leave behind

all forms and structures of the past, to make the bet of faith, to risk encounter with chaos, to leap over the walls which offer protection, and to live without the certainties of the past. Prayer is in truth the continual re-committal of a person to the migrant life.

This describes well the kind of venture that our converts described above have undertaken. We are called to such a journey to freedom through continuous conversion.

Readers' response

- Reflect on the occasions when you have been an Abraham or a Sarah, in however humble a way; when you have been able to say yes to 'a voice' beckoning you. Were you able to sustain your choice? Reflect also on when you have been like the rich young person. What prevented you going forward? Do those issues still afflict you?

- Consider the definitions of conversion in this chapter. Which do you prefer and why? What would be your definition?

- Have you known people who have converted between faiths, or between faith and atheism? What have been the reasons for their decision – religious, personal, psychological, socio-logical? If you know any of these people now, you may want to talk with them. Do you feel that for them conversion has meant freedom?

- What has been your personal story of conversion? Reflect on your own life, in relation to the link between conversion and liberation.

Passages for meditation

Henri Nouwen, *Bread for the Journey*, p.24:

Optimism and hope are radically different attitudes. Opti-mism is the expectation that things – the weather, human relationships, the economy, the political situation, and so on – will get better. Hope is the trust that God will fulfil God's promises to us in a way that leads us to true freedom. The optimist speaks about concrete changes in the future. The person of hope lives in the moment, with the knowledge and trust that all of life is in good hands. All the great spiritual leaders in history were people of hope. Abraham, Moses, Ruth, Mary, Jesus, Rumi, Gandhi and Dorothy Day all lived with a promise in their hearts that guided them towards a future without the need to know exactly what it would look like. Let's live with hope.

Bread for the Journey, p.270:

God says, 'I am offering you life or death, blessing or curse. Choose life, then, so that you and your descendants may live' (Deuteronomy 30:19). 'Choose life', that's God's call for us, and there is not a moment in which we do not have to make a choice. Life and death are always before us. In our imaginations, our thoughts, our words, our gestures, our actions . . . even in our non-actions. This choice for life starts in a very interior place. Underneath very life-affirming behaviour I can still harbour death-thoughts and death-feelings. The most important questions is not 'Do I kill?' but 'Do I carry a blessing in my heart or a curse?' The bullet that kills is only the final instrument of the hatred that began in the heart long before the gun was picked up.

Dietrich Bonhoeffer, *The Cost of Discipleship,* pp.69–70:

Jesus may have said: 'Sell thy goods,' but he meant: 'Do not let it be a matter of consequence to you that you have outward prosperity; rather keep your goods quietly, having them as if you had them not. Let not your heart be in your goods.' We are excusing ourselves from single-minded obedience to the word of Jesus on the pretext of legalism and a supposed preference for an obedience 'in faith'. The difference between ourselves and the rich young man is that he was not allowed to solace his regrets by saying, 'Never mind what Jesus says, I can still hold on to my riches, but in a spirit of inner detachment. Despite my inadequacy I can take comfort in the thought that God has forgiven my sins and I can have fellowship with Christ in faith.' But no, he went away sorrowful. Because he would not obey, he could not believe. In this the young man was quite honest. He went away from Jesus and indeed this honesty had more promise than any apparent communion with Jesus based on disobedience.

Chapter 6

FREEDOM TO CHOOSE: FREEDOM AND RESPONSIBILITY

Deuteronomy 30:15–20; John 6:59–71

> I call heaven and earth to witness against you today, that I have set before you life and death, blessings and curses. Choose life so that you and your descendants may live.
>
> *Deuteronomy 30:19*

> Simon Peter answered him, 'Lord, to whom can we go? You have the words of eternal life.'
>
> *John 6:68*

Joe was a middle-aged man who made the choice to leave the alcoholism that was enslaving him and depriving him of any sense of freedom. This choice was about what he would not do; equally important was a further decision, to fill the vacuum in his life by working for alienated youth near his home in the tenements of inner-city Glasgow. He began to use his football skill to develop a local youth team. This meant a great commitment of time, as he encouraged the team in regular training sessions. He found himself increasingly identifying with a young drug addict. Joe hoped that football would help release the addict from his addiction, as well as helping his girlfriend, also an addict. At the same time, Joe developed a friendship with a middle-class woman working in the area. He fell deeply in love with her. This is the scenario we face in the film *My Name Is Joe*.

One day Joe found himself facing a stark choice. The young couple were being threatened by a gang, and were facing serious reprisals if they did not go to a rendezvous to pick up a consignment of drugs. They were paralysed with fear, and could not do it. They waited for the consequences. To protect them, Joe chose to collect the package himself. He made this choice at the cost of his own happiness, because his girlfriend said clearly that she could not remain with someone who was involved in drug-running. Joe chose the way that he believed would save the young people and enable them to be released from the trap they had found themselves in. Everything went wrong, not only did Joe lose his girl, but the young man hanged himself. The film ends with Joe's return to drink.

It is a dark tragedy, made all the worse by the darkness of the context, a barren sector of the inner city, a kind of Golgotha. Joe seemed to me a Christ-like figure, in some respects. He made the choice to identify with the excluded, those who had no hope. He gave his life in an attempt to free them, to save them and give them dignity. All this was at the cost of his own happiness. He gave his life in a real sense for others. And he did this at the cost, in some ways, of his own principles. There was no way that he could remain 'clean', in the oppressive context in which he had been placed. I am reminded of Bonhoeffer's agonising choice to go against his long-held pacifist principles, 'to be made sin for Christ's sake', as he agreed to join the plot to kill Hitler in an attempt to save his nation and the Jews in particular.

It is often in the face of great tragedy that choice comes to us. Do we choose to remain locked into the circumstances which have brought us tragedy, or do we make a choice to move on and find life again? One of my theological students described why he chose to offer himself for the ordained ministry. His vocation came, remarkably, out of the experience of returning home one day to find his young son hanged in the garden, as a result of a freak accident. The rope from a tree swing had become caught round his neck. He could not be revived. Such an experience could have resulted in total destruction of the parents' Christian faith; how could a good God allow this to happen to an innocent child? But in fact after a traumatic period of suffering and self-punishment, this became the spur to a sense of calling. The loss of this life became a challenge to the man to give up a senior, well-paid job to offer life to others through ordained ministry within the church.

Bereavements often confront us with such choices. Can we go on living? Can we find a new purpose in life? Or will we become locked into what has happened? Will we cling to the past?

Medieval painters were fascinated by the story of the encounter in the garden on Easter morning between Mary Magdalene and the risen Lord Jesus, recorded in John chapter 20. 'Supposing him to be the gardener' is how Mary, at first glance, mistakes the one to whom she has dedicated her life and who is standing in front of her. As he addresses her by name, she realises who it is: 'Rabboni', 'Master' and then come the pivotal words as she reaches out to him in her astonishment, her joy, her fear – 'Do not touch me', 'I am not yet ascended to the Father . . . to your God and my God.' There is a series of paintings with the title 'Noli me tangere', and they portray Jesus always with a hoe, as he holds himself at arm's length from the woman who longs to touch him, the woman who reaches out to him in love. We feel Jesus' compassion and intensity of gaze, but also the constraint he is under to move on.

The problem with Mary's clinging to him was that she would thereby prevent him becoming available to all, as the resurrected Lord. At the same time, she would prevent herself from moving on, from becoming what God had called her to be, from becoming the first witness to the miracle of the resurrection, as she went to the frightened disciples and told them, 'I have seen the Lord!'

The disciples together were to face such a choice after the ascension. Were they to remain where they were on the mountain, gazing up into heaven? Or would they choose to go to Jerusalem, to wait, to be open to what might happen to them there? They chose to move on and were therefore given the

Pentecost experience and the energy to fulfil the challenge they had been given, 'to make disciples of all nations'.

When my mother died suddenly of a stroke in 1992, my father had had no time to prepare for her death. She had earlier given instructions to be cremated, but in the days before the funeral he found this very difficult to accept. How could he let go so finally of the person he had loved for 50 years? Somehow he was led to this passage in John, which enabled him to release himself, and indeed to release her. She was not gone for ever, but risen into something infinitely greater. He had to offer her freedom, and bear his own freedom. He found also a letter from my mother, in which she explained that life in physical pain since her first stroke had become a real struggle and that she was tired. She was ready to go whenever that happened, and that her love for her family would abide for ever. She was sure that we would meet again in some way in the future, in God's closer presence. In the face of death, there has to be a freedom to let go, a freedom to be let go, so that the miracle of receiving back can ultimately happen. The choice at first is merely to go on living, accepting that grief is a form of loving. The next stage is about how we can rediscover ourselves, which may well only be possible as we give ourselves to others.

Anthony Bloom puts such a choice memorably in this passage entitled 'Modern man faces death':[1]

> With every person who dies, part of us is already in eternity. We must let go of everything that was small, that was separation, alienation and estrangement, and reach out to that serenity and greatness, newness and abundance of life into which the departed person has entered. We should not speak of our love in the past tense. Love is a thing that does not fade in a faithful heart. It does not go into the past unless we betray our love. We must keep our love alive in a new situation, as actively and creatively, and more so, more often, than when the person was with us. Our love cannot be dead because a person has died. If that is true, our life must be a continuation of theirs, with all its significance. We must reflect on all that was beauty, and nobility,

in that person, and make sure those around us, and our surroundings, do not lose anything through the death. This applies to all families and friends as well as the immediate bereaved, so that the seed that has fallen into corruption may give a hundredfold harvest in the hearts and lives of others.

One thing is at the front, with every bereaved person – the sense of separation, of being left alone. One has to accept it creatively and to say, 'I have a double task to fulfil – the dead person's work and my own. I must be great for two, reveal integrity for two.

Such a challenge is particularly difficult for those who have been very close. Two examples I have known. A priest who had been involved throughout his ministry with people of other faiths, died suddenly. His widow made a conscious decision, as a way of moving forward from the shock, that she would visit a person of another faith every day throughout the Lenten season. After a further period, she made another decision, to offer herself for overseas service, something they had done for many years as a couple, and more recently had wanted to do again, but it had not worked out. This was one person choosing to live for two.

In another case, a missionary couple, Bill and Margaret, gave their whole life to India, as theological teachers. In the last years of their ministry, both said yes to enormous challenges that came to them, and in this way were able to offer 'life' to many lost ones. Bill one day visited the prison, next to the new seminary where he was teaching. He was allowed into the prison, and without escort felt free to roam around. He began visiting prisoners in single cells, who, he discovered, were those awaiting execution. He talked with them and wrote down their names for prayer. After a week, he asked to go to visit again. He was told this time that he could only visit people by name. He had the names. So began a remarkable ministry throughout the prison, and in particular to those condemned to death.

I inherited this ministry when Bill retired, and in the period of overlap I was privileged to witness the baptism of a prisoner who was executed three days later. He had killed his father in a family quarrel. Bill spent much time with him, and offered him the choice of dying in his guilt and sadness or of choosing life. He told the man of a God who in Jesus Christ would forgive even one like him, as he had said to the thief beside him on the cross, 'Today you will be with me in paradise.' The prisoner had previously thought that all that had happened to him was inevitable, part of his bad 'karma', according to the popular Hindu belief system. He was introduced to the story of Nicodemus in John, chapter 3, where the Pharisee was offered the choice of coming out of darkness into the light and being born again. Enigmatically, in that chapter we do not learn whether Nicodemus had the courage to make that choice. But the offer is there for all people, and this prisoner wanted to respond.

He took baptism through the prison bars because there was not time to get the necessary permission for his release from the cell. He insisted on water baptism, not baptism by desire, which would have been easier. He knew the story in John 3 by then: 'I want to be in the kingdom, I need the water.' 'Unless you are born again of water and the spirit, you will not enter the kingdom of heaven.' He took the baptism name of Arul (Grace), in the Tamil language, rather than 'Barabbas', which he had first requested because he had killed someone. 'You are a forgiven sinner like all of us,' he was told. When he had been baptised kneeling, he stood up and embraced me through the bars, bare-chested, as the condemned prisoners were. I asked him how he felt. He replied '*Perinbon*' ('I am in bliss'). His eyes were shining with joy, and he felt that as a Christian he must do something for others, as a sign of his baptism. He signed a document, giving his eyes to another after he died, so that they might see again. As he was hanged, it seemed as though his head was resting upon his Lord: 'Come unto me all you who are heavy laden, and I will give you rest.' His body was taken to his village and a cross raised over his grave, the first ever to be seen in that village. He witnessed even beyond his death. He chose life, though faced with certain death.

Meanwhile, Margaret was faced with no less a challenge. She used to visit the women's prison, where young women were imprisoned for prostitution, a way of life they had usually entered out of dire poverty, or because they had been 'captured' by male brothel keepers. One day one of the women said to Margaret, 'Amma, I don't want to go back to that life. Help me.' Margaret was about two years from retirement, when most people would have chosen an easier life. But Margaret agreed to meet the woman at the prison gate, and took her to her own home before the brothel owner could recapture her. She took her to the seminary, and soon another girl followed. Bill put his foot down when two more wished to come. But Margaret did not give up, nor was she satisfied with a short-term solution. She begged the principal to give her a college house so that she could begin to form a small community, for which she took responsibility. Eventually there were over 20 women living within the seminary, and a separate site had to be found for a larger home, to become known as 'Arulagam', 'Place of Grace'. Here the possibility of new life has been offered to many girls over the 20 years of the home's existence. Some do not choose a new life, of course, but merely a rest before returning to their profession. But many have moved on to live positive lives, both in terms of their work and their family situation. Now a second institution has been founded for those suffering from AIDS. In both places, those whom the world counts as nothing or even less have found some dignity and love. This was all because a senior woman chose a hard, but deeply fulfilling path.

Bill and Margaret retired to a south coast town where a well-wisher, having heard of their work, lent them a bungalow to live in. When I visited, I was not surprised to hear that their local church had become a centre for several causes focusing on questions of social justice, peace and international development, and that Margaret was behind most of them. Margaret eventually died of cancer, and here Bill faced a challenge like that suggested in the passage above from Anthony Bloom.

He was himself weak and confined to living in a home. He had always had a somewhat depressive personality, which he had fought against, with Margaret's crucial help. Now he could easily have chosen to turn his face to the wall and die. But he made a decision to continue to live for others, as Margaret had done supremely. He became a pastoral support to many in his home, and when the Decade of Evangelism was declared, he mobilised a few of the more able-bodied to go out into the estate around the home, to call on the houses, and to play their part in sharing the love of Jesus Christ. This, in a different context, was what he had tried to do in the prison.

Bill's and Margaret's whole Christian lives had centred upon being free to make bold choices. They never said 'this is how things are and so this is how they must remain'; they responded repeatedly to the call to do what they could where they were.

Another group who are faced with the deep challenge of choice are those who are struck down suddenly by some form of illness or handicap. In such circumstances, do we choose to become bitter at life's unfairness, mournful about what we have lost and paralysed about the future? Or can we make a choice to accept what has happened and to live for the future? The choice is ours alone and no one else can make it for us.

Our daughter Joanna, mentioned earlier in chapter 4, has made such choices on an almost daily basis since she suffered her stroke. She has had to face a struggle at all levels of her life, to learn afresh all that she had lost, to rebuild her life and sense of self-worth, and to regain an element of confidence. She has had to build up new networks of friends, since she quickly lost all those who had known her before and who, seemingly, had not the patience to accompany her on the journey of rehabilitation. She has made choices about when to depend on her family, and when to assert her necessary need for freedom. At any point she could have given up. Life has been often very tiring, and the system set against her at every point. But gradually year by year there has been progress. She qualified in photography. She also found she could be a counsellor to other and more recent young stroke victims. She challenged them to look forward with hope, and not be locked into the past, enchained by what had happened.

How we make the major choices of our life may vary, depending on our personality, the way we make decisions anyway, the nature of the choice and how we prioritise, as well as the influence of those around us. We may be the kind of person who weighs all the options and calculates how many reasons there are for a choice and how many against, and the respective weight of those reasons. We may be the kind of person who writes lists. I remember enabling such an exercise with someone who had been asked to be a bishop in a very difficult context in Africa. Or we may be someone for whom intuition is the driving force. We have a hunch that a particular path is right, and we go for it; the reasons are then used to back it, to explain it. Sometimes we are left feeling we have no choice because of the strong influence of another. An ordained friend told me that his calling was from a particular bishop, who said, 'The church in our place needs you. You should be ordained.' In retrospect he felt he had no choice; but in the event he did not respond until well after the bishop's death. He in fact had chosen the timing.

How we prioritise varies, depending on the choice involved. How to balance vocation and family is a regular dilemma for a Christian. When I was at theological college, I remember being told that the greatest problem for a married priest was perpetual guilt – guilt when they are at home because they should be with others, and guilt when they are with others that they should be at home. The guide said that the choices were ours and ours alone, and that we must do what we felt right in the situation, not what others imposed upon our over-exercised conscience. One choice my wife and I made was to return to Britain from India, making our children's future education the priority rather than the work we were very committed to. Most agreed with us, but when the decision was taken, one colleague said he was sorry we had made this decision. We had learned the language and culture, and were doing a very good job, we should have found some other way, he argued.

This question nagged at me. Had we really decided aright? I was much helped by going to discuss it with a retired missionary bishop. He began weeping, and said, 'You have chosen rightly.' He told us that he had not seen his daughter for several years, and he remembered the time he had lost her. She had been going off to boarding school, and he took her to the station. He got involved in church business on the platform with some people who saw an opportunity to talk to him. He realised what he had come for too late. The train was going beyond the long platform, and all he could see was the hand of his daughter in the distance, trying to catch his attention with a desperate wave.

We can probably only be sure of the rightness or otherwise of any particular choice in retrospect; nor will we ever know the outcome if we had made a different choice. Life is not like the film *Sliding Doors*, which shows two stories – the one that happens if a young woman catches the tube, the other if she finds the doors closed. Spiritually, only as we look back can we see how the Holy Spirit has worked in our lives. As was said by Meryl Streep in another film, *The Bridges of Madison County*, in some ways 'we are the choices we have made,' but we can still adjust those choices if appropriate, or enable them to work for good, as St Paul believes can happen, if we truly focus upon the God who calls us and is with us.

The Bible is in some ways the history of choices that people have made. It is also the history of God's interaction with his people. Here is the theological paradox of freedom and choice. At one level, individuals, and indeed the nation, choose freely. That is the basis of responsibility. If there is not freedom of choice, there is no objective responsibility. We may feel responsible, but that is a purely subjective feeling. Because we could do no other, responsibility lies elsewhere. This applies in ethics and every other area of life. We need to be punished for wrongdoing, but that is in order to protect society, or to bring change to our way of acting or personality. It is not because we should face the consequences of our actions.

If we hold such a view, we may name the constraining force that means we are not objectively free as fate. 'I could do no other.' 'I couldn't help it.' 'When you have got to go, you've got to go.' 'That was his fate.' 'We must just grin and bear it, we have no choice.' 'She was born like that.' Such observations indicate a whole attitude to life that can be termed 'fatalistic'. This can apply also to wider reflections, for example, about nations and their behaviour. 'Northern Ireland will always be a mess.' 'That's how Africa is, nothing can be done about it, it is a basket case.' 'Class conflict is inevitable.'

A popular understanding of this kind of attitude has been given a pseudo-religious form in recent years by the use of the word 'karma'. 'That is his karma.' This term gained notoriety when used by the England football manager at the time, Glenn Hoddle, who applied it to his philosophy of life. Often it is linked to a belief in reincarnation, that 'what you sow in this life, you reap in the next.' This has an attraction, but at its worst can become a closed and deterministic system. It can lead to an attitude that means we do nothing about how things are because there is nothing much we can change, whether in individuals, communities or in wider movements of history.

I remember a discussion with the Hindu superintendent of the prison mentioned earlier. He asked why we Christians spent so much time talking with and helping individual prisoners and their families, as part of our prison ministry. We replied that we believed that each person could change, if they received love, care and teaching and could begin to believe in themselves again. He answered that this was a pointless task, and one that cost us great toil unnecessarily: 'For they are what they are, that is their karma. They must just work things through. You would be better using your money, in giving them all a feast a few times a year. This would enable you to improve your own karma, for much less effort. You would gain from the fruits of such good actions, without it costing you so much toil which would in the end be fruitless.' Our reply here was to explain that, in our understanding, each of these individuals had been made in God's image and was redeemable as such. Christ had died for each of them, as for us. Through repentance and forgiveness they could find new life. All is not inevitable.

There are much more subtle understandings of karma, which is a key concept in Eastern philosophy. But this is how it was being interpreted in a popular way. It was an interpretation such as this that led at one time to leaving those suffering from leprosy to their fate, as indeed with those suffering from today's leprosy, AIDS. There is no real interventionist action we can take which will alter the inevitable outcome, it is argued, so let us do something else with our time.

In the Indian prison, there was a prisoner awaiting execution. He was apathetic and accepting of the inevitable, as he moved from cell to cell, nearer to the end of the row. Those nearest to execution were at the end of the line. The stages of moving from one end to the other might take years, depending on the process of appeals. 'Progress' took place either because someone was executed or because someone had a sentence commuted to life imprisonment and they stepped out into the main prison. Both groups vacated cells. This particular prisoner accepted his fate because it was as a result of his karma, he felt. He had carried out a brutal murder and felt no guilt at all. It had happened because he had fulfilled what had to be done within his caste duties.

In the next cell was a staunch Christian. The two used to talk through their bars. The Christian suggested to his neighbour that he might find help through reading the Bible. He arranged for a visiting sister to offer him one. Though most prisoners rejected such a gift, and some mocked the giver, this man accepted it. His neighbour guided him to Psalm 51. Here, as he reflected at length, he learned of sin, responsibility and personal guilt.

He learned too of a personal God, and one who would forgive even him, if he turned to him with the prayer set out in verse 1: 'Have mercy on me, O God, according to your steadfast love; according to your abundant mercy blot out my transgressions.' And in verse 10: 'Create in me a clean heart, O God, and put a new and right spirit within me.' He was brought face to face with what he had done: 'For I know my transgressions, and my sin is ever before me' (v.3). He realised the long history which had made him what he is: 'I was born guilty, a sinner when my mother conceived me'(v.5). What is needed is repentance of the heart: 'The sacrifice acceptable to God is a broken spirit, a broken and contrite heart you will not despise' (v.17). For the first time he felt a freedom of choice. God was open to him. His compassion was infinite. He needed to understand the depth of his sin, and turn to God. This was not a gloomy affair, rather it was a joyful acknowledgement of God's grace: 'Lord, open my lips, and my mouth will declare your praise' (v.15).

The conclusion to this story is that the Christian neighbouring prisoner was in fact executed, while the new believer had his sentence reduced to life imprisonment. In his further decade in prison, he became a witness to others, as his neighbour had been to him. He was a very good singer in classical South Indian style, and he wrote a number of songs focusing on his experience of his new sense of freedom, enabled by the grace of his God. Such a story was not the norm, but is representative of several I encountered, and is found in prisons throughout the world, where people are faced with real starkness of choice.

From the early chapters of Genesis, the Bible wrestles with the question of freedom and responsibility. The stories of Adam and Eve, and their choice to eat the apple, assume that this choice was free. So too does the story of Cain and Abel and the rhetorical answer given by Cain to God's question about the whereabouts of Abel, whom Cain has killed: 'Am I my brother's keeper?' Of course he is his brother's keeper, that is why Cain is punished to become a wanderer on the earth. We are responsible for the good and evil we do to our brother and sister. It is the same with the punishment of humanity at the time of the great flood, and the wilfulness of that same humanity as they build the tower of Babel and try to reach up to God (ch.11). There is an assertion of the possibility of wilfulness and the making of wrong choices. It is not just a matter of karma.

In the history of Israel the wrongdoings of kings and leaders are seen as leading to the suffering of the whole people. The assertion that we suffer for the sins of our fathers and grandfathers, to the second and third generations, takes a similar view. In a limited way, people may feel they are inheriting bad karma from what has gone before. But it is clear that that karma has been produced by individual disobedient action for which a king or someone else has been responsible. And it is possible to reverse what seems inevitable. Hence the desperate urgency of the messages of the prophets. This is how things are, but they need not be so: repent and begin again.

The fact that some were saying that nothing could be done was the reason for the challenge of both Jeremiah and Ezekiel: when we eat sour grapes, it is our own teeth that are set on edge, not those of our fathers or our children. We are free to eat or not, and are responsible for what happens. Of course such actions have consequences. If I drink to excess, my family will suffer and may disintegrate. Abused children so often carry the conse-

quences of the choices of others. There is a likelihood that they
in turn will abuse those who come under their influence. But
there is no inevitability about this, if we take a biblical view.
There are great difficulties, but the chain of consequence can be
broken.

In the Old Testament, it is not just individuals but the Jewish
nation as a whole that has choices before it. It is free to choose
life or death. As they were about to enter the promised land,
which Moses knew he himself would never enter, he challenged
them with the choice that he believed God was offering them:
'Today I offer you the choice of life and good, or death and evil.'
The choice of life was in their hearts, not high in the heavens or
across the seas. The choice was to conform to God's ways and
to keep his commandments, which Moses believed were written
on their hearts. The choice was not predetermined, and had to
be repeated again and again at crucial points in their history.
God's covenantal promise is clear: he will be with them, but they
must choose to play their part.

Such choices continue to face nations, where recent history
belies the idea that everything is inevitable. Perhaps the most
dramatic example is South Africa, which changed because certain
individuals began a movement for change. Apartheid seemed
insurmountable, set in stone. All the power seemed to be stacked
against those who did not accept this inevitability and who suggested there was a continuing choice before South Africa and its
people. Trevor Huddleston asserted that nothing so evil and
blasphemous as apartheid could go on. What was needed was
for Christian people to rise from their pews and stand together.
His pupil Desmond Tutu was characterised by this sense of hope.
'I know things will change, for God is good.' 'We will be free.'
This could only have happened because people made choices
towards change. Nelson Mandela's genius as a leader was to give
white people a choice – not between sell-out and self-destruction,
but between continuing fear and a new South Africa, a rainbow
nation, that would offer them a place with the black people they
had oppressed. He offered a 'win-win' situation, where people
really had a choice for life, and there were enough open minds
to make such a choice, painful as it was.

But behind these two giants, there were countless 'little ones' who kept hope alive and made their own 'little' choices, which together allowed the possibility of the great choice. Three such persons, all women, I met in South Africa. One was Gertrude, the least well known of them. She was an ordinary black Christian social worker in Pietermaritzberg. I stayed one night with her in 1992. This was during the most violent of times in the death throes of apartheid. The Group Areas Act had been repealed, and for the first time for decades black people could go to live in white areas. She felt challenged to go to live in an Afrikaan street. Friends supported her and enabled her financially to move into this lonely and exposed place. She was sure that this was where the Lord was leading her; someone had to be first. The quiet courage of this little woman was infectious, and I was happy to go with her to a downtown area I had been told by others it was dangerous to be in. She took me also to the railway station and showed me, with enormous respect, the place where before the First World War Gandhi had been thrown off a train because of the colour of his skin. This was the incident that led him to take up non-violent struggle, an instrument he perfected on his return to India. When I met Gertrude again in 1997, she was still maintaining her faith in life and in the goodness of God, though she also recounted the recent deaths by violence of two in her family.

Another was Mahatma Gandhi's granddaughter, whom we met in Durban. She had seen the destruction of her life's work, which had been to rebuild the Phoenix settlement outside the city, where her grandfather had had an *ashram* and built up a printing press. It had been destroyed in 'black on black' violence, as it was then known, in the 1980s. But rather than give up in resignation, she took us to the settlement site, and showed us where she was working with different communities, to enable the place to become a symbol of multi-racial hope in the area. There had been setbacks, but she was full of the inspiring spirit of her illustrious forebear and was sure that a new Phoenix would rise from the ashes.

The third was an Afrikaan woman, Tish, who married across the white divide, her husband being of British descent. Together

they founded Wilgerspruit, a community which P. W. Botha
famously described as 'a den of vipers'. There were numerous
projects within this foundation, all challenging the roots of apartheid. But the most striking and costly perspective of all was their
personal choice to defy the Group Areas Act, and to adopt a
whole family of children, of every race and mixture of races,
a kind of 'rainbow nation' in advance. Their 'children', nearer
to twenty than ten, as I remember, lived in community with the
couple and their two natural daughters. Tish lived under perpetual
stress, both at home, in her enabling of the projects, and through
the even greater physical danger she faced when she moved out
of the compound into the alien world around her. She lived on
her nerves, a life of great intensity and with great warmth to
those who, like me, used to visit. She typified for me, when I
stayed there, an indomitable spirit, determined to choose life, for
herself, those she believed in, and in the end for her nation.

Recent decades have seen such corporate choices before
nations in quite dramatic ways. Europe faced them in 1945, as
it viewed its own self-destruction. Was the story of the years
after 1918 to be repeated in the ensuing years? Whatever the
form that European union has taken, and that is still much under
debate, the choice for peace and solidarity between the nations
of Western Europe has been a major miracle in the light of the
history not just of the first half of the twentieth century, but of
earlier centuries marked by war and division. The choice made
by Mikhail Gorbachev to end the division between the Eastern
bloc and Western Europe, and to allow people power to dismantle
both the Iron Curtain and the Berlin Wall, was perhaps an even
greater miracle.

That miracle can be witnessed in many places, of which I
mention just two that I have visited. The Iron Curtain began to
be dismantled in Hungary in 1989. I visited Budapest in 2001,
and it was hard to believe how much could have happened in
just twelve years. I went to the sculpture park, which is out
beyond the city boundaries. This is not contemporary art or
sculpture from the heyday of the Austro-Hungarian Empire.
Rather it is an open-air collection of enormous pieces from the
Communist period. They are representations in socialist-realist

style, so like that of the Nazi period – enormous memorials to the labouring masses, the Communist workers, to Marx and Lenin, and to their local equivalents in Budapest. The preservation of these sculptures, here in Eastern Europe, is a stark reminder of the choice that was made in 1989 and its speedy implementation. It is striking that the newest of the statues is from a date not long before 1989.

Equally moving was a visit I made to Lithuania in 2000. Here in Vilnius I saw a number of memorials. One was the KGB prison, now a grim museum, which was described as the most direct way to Siberia. Another was a commemoration of the vast human chain that had stretched in 1991 from Tallinn in Estonia to Vilnius, demanding that the Soviets withdrew from their occupation. This they did at the cost of the few who had died as they took over the radio station, and there was a memorial to these people. All are memorials to those who were sure that we do have choices before us, and that all is not inevitable. Behind these momentous choices made by nations, there are the countless choices made by individuals to join movements that eventually bring about dramatic change, maybe after many years of patient struggle.

Many more critical choices lie before us if the world is to be a more peaceful place, not least the choices facing leaders in such places as Northern Ireland, Israel/Palestine, the Congo, Sri Lanka. Here the division is between those who feel that conflict is inevitable and that history is irreversible, and those who can see the realities of the situation, but believe that the choice of life is possible, even in these darkest of contexts. I was part of a peace solidarity visit to Sri Lanka from the British Churches in 1999. Over 60,000 people, Tamils, Sinhala and Muslims, have died in the civil conflict there. I also witnessed the discussions in a cross-cultural group of Sri Lankans in the West Midlands, who met regularly for nearly two years. Both on the island itself and in our group in Birmingham, who were a microcosm of that island, there were clear divisions along religious and racial grounds, which were predictable, but there was also another major division which ran across these barriers. On the one hand there were those who were dominated by past history, believing

that things had at one time been liveable with, but that the forces
of history and past mistakes and misunderstandings were so
strong that endless conflict and division was the only realistic
expectation. A running sore was the most that could be hoped
for. Then there were others who did not dispute the historical
realities or the contemporary context, but who believed that the
human spirit would not be quenched, and that in time a miracle
of transformation could take place, that would bring life again
to this beautiful island. These were the ones who were prepared to work for peace, in small steps maybe, but with hope
rather than optimism. These were the ones who asserted that our
group, unusual in itself in that it contained Tamil, Sinhala and
Muslim who were prepared to own their feelings and to talk
from the heart as well as the head, was itself a sign of choice
for life and hope, and must make a difference, at least in the
lives of those who were meeting.

At the Sri Lankan end, there were those who had been working
away at peace and justice projects, appearing to the outsider as
small and struggling, but who were sustained by an abiding sense
of this choice for life. There are those like the University Teachers
Association, who are prepared literally to face death because of
their stance which is equally critical of both sides in the conflict.
They remind me of Jeremiah, as they continually face personal
suffering, unpopularity and danger for what they believe is truth's
sake. There are all the numerous ordinary people on all sides
who are just war weary and long for peace, and no longer want
endless choices towards death. It is perhaps this kind of mass
feeling that is the most hopeful sign, paradoxically – things are
as they are but cannot go on like this forever.

Some make a choice as individuals, against the way the masses
are leading them, and these are perhaps the most courageous
choices of all. The so-called righteous Gentiles can stand for this
category. These are those who made a decision, often at the cost
of their lives, to shelter Jewish people during the Nazi period or
to enable them to escape. I heard an unsolicited testimony to one
when in Budapest. We were being shown round the biggest
Jewish synagogue in Eastern Europe, one that has risen from the
ashes of the Hungarian Jewish community, which had survived

until 1944 and then been systematically deported to extermination camps at record speed, as the war neared its end. A small minority survived, and those who have remained in Budapest, or returned there, have rebuilt this great synagogue, a sign of their hope for the future. Our guide was a Jewish layman aged about sixty, but who looked older. He took us through the rest of the museum and then to the history of the 1940s. He explained that all his family had died, but he had survived, because, he said quietly, of the brave choice of one man. He pointed to a photograph of Walendorf, the Swedish ambassador, who had saved twenty thousand people, including himself as a young boy, by packing them into his embassy compound and granting them immediate exit visas, with Swedish protection.

There is a similar testimony in Vilnius to the Japanese ambassador, who had enabled thousands to escape the 'Jerusalem of northern Europe' in similar fashion. At Yad Vashem, the memorial to the *Shoah* (the Hebrew word for Holocaust) in Jerusalem, most striking is the plantation of trees around it. Each has been given a different plaque, and they are memorials to individual 'righteous Gentiles'. Schindler is there, the best-known of many. His moral character, as is well known, was ambiguous, to say the least. But in the face of a choice about life and death for thousands of Jews, he chose life. The stories behind all the other plaques would no doubt reveal equally the choices people have made for life, even at the cost of their own lives.

The book *Dying We Live* is a powerful testimony, in the form of a collection of last letters, to those who gave their lives in resistance to Hitler.[2] These letters are a remarkable testimony to faith in God and the human spirit, and to people's certainty that in the end, 'We know that everything works for good for those who love him, who are called according to his purpose.' They are a testimony indeed to the whole of Romans 8, and especially verses 24 and 25: 'For in this hope we were saved. Now hope that is seen is not hope. For who hopes for what he sees? But if we hope for what we do not see, we wait for it with patience.' So also the resounding faith of verse 38: 'For I am sure that neither death, nor life, nor angels, nor principalities, nor things present, nor things to come, nor powers, nor height, nor depth,

nor anything else in all creation, will be able to separate us from
the love of God in Christ Jesus our Lord.'

In some ways, these martyrs mirror the kind of choices Jesus
made, as they faced death on behalf of others. In Mark's gospel,
from chapter 3 onwards, Jesus faced death, as people began to
plot against him, to kill him. The occasion had been his insistence
that he should heal a man with a withered arm on the Sabbath.
Fear of such plots, fear of death, did not make him choose the
way of safety when the challenge to do good was in front of
him. From the experience on the Mount of Transfiguration
onwards (ch.8), he set his face to Jerusalem, well aware of the
risks as he headed straight into conflict and possible death. The
picture is especially clear in 10:32: 'They were on the road going
up to Jerusalem, and Jesus was walking ahead of them. The
disciples were amazed, and those who followed were afraid.' He
made further choices towards death, as he entered the gates of
the city, as he cast out the money-changers from the temple, as
he let Judas go out into the night, as he forbade Peter to use his
sword to defend his master. In Gethsemane, all was focused on
the prayer that the cup of suffering and death might pass from
him, but what was ultimate was what was God's will. Jesus went
forward to his trial, mocking, persecution and death. All the
worst was thrown at him, when as Vanstone says in *The Stature
of Waiting,* he was pushed from place to place. He says less and
less, as he appears to be losing control, and where his choices
seem to be at an end.

Yet, paradoxically, he affirms his very freedom as he cannot
be deflected from the way forward. He took upon his shoulders,
not just the physical weight of the cross, but the hatred of the
powers of this world and the sadness of the cowardice of his
disciples, as he continued to face forward. On the cross itself,
he faced also a deep sense of loneliness, where he felt forsaken
even by God, as he cried out 'My God, my God, why hast thou
forsaken me?' And yet this moment of fear and abandonment
became a moment when he finally overcame death, as he freely
chose to trust in the promises of that same God, that victory over
death would be his. And through that victory, death would
become a gift for all humanity, as it became the path to eternal

life and freedom: 'O death, where is thy victory, oh death, where is thy sting?', 'Death's mightiest powers have done their worst . . .'

In the second passage mentioned at the beginning of the chapter, the disciples in the fourth gospel were offered a clear choice – to follow on this journey or go back to the safety of their former lives. The majority chose to go back. Such is always likely to be the case in the face of tough decisions. The twelve chose to go on, seemingly out of a sense of resignation – 'To whom shall we go?' – but also out of a realisation that only by such a choice, a choice for death, can they find eternal life.

Such a choice needs to be taken, not once but daily, as the journey goes on. As Jesus puts it in Luke's gospel (9:23–4), 'Anyone who wants to be a follower of mine must renounce self; day after day, he must take up his cross, and follow me. Whoever wants to save his life will lose it, but whoever loses his life for my sake will save it.' Most of my illustrations in this chapter are not about a single choice, though that may be involved; they are about a long haul, often over many years, of a reaffirming of that choice, whether it is the choice before individuals or before communities or nations. Humanity seems to have an incorrigible tendency to step backwards, if left to itself. That is a reason why the Lucan version of this passage is most helpful. Mark and Matthew suggest a one-off choice, ' . . . let him take up his cross and follow me'. Only Luke adds the word 'daily'. This is the challenge of the freedom we have been given now. It is daily that we are called to take up the challenges that are before us. As Dag Hammarskjöld expresses it, in a fitting message to leave with the reader at the end of these meditations:[3]

> Do not look back. And do not dream about the future either. It will neither give you back the past, nor satisfy your other day-dreams. Your duty, your reward – your destiny – are *here* and *now*.

Or:[4]

> Lead us not into temptation,
> But deliver us from evil:
> Let all that is in me serve Thee,
> And *thus* free me from all fear.
> You dare your *Yes* – and experience a meaning.
> You repeat your Yes – and all things acquire a meaning.
> When everything has a meaning, how can you live anything
>   but a *Yes*.

Readers' response

- Reflect on your life and how you have come to be where you are now. At what points in particular did you choose to say *Yes* to life? Are you faced with any significant choices at this point?

- Have there been times when you chose to say *No*? What influenced you? Are you able to review any of those decisions, in the light of changed circumstances, or because you have moved on?

- What significant choices do you think our society, the nation, or the global community, is facing at the present time? Is there anything you can do to contribute to that choice?

- Give thanks for anyone you have known who has faced a great tragedy or loss and affirmed their life through it and beyond, and moved on.

Passages for meditation

Henri Nouwen, *Bread for the Journey*, p.14:

> Choices. Choices make a difference. Two people are in the same accident and are severely wounded. They did not choose to be in the accident. It happened to them. But one of them chose to live the experience in bitterness,

the other in gratitude. These choices radically influence their lives and the lives of their families and friends. We have very little control over what happens in our lives, but we have a lot of control over how we integrate and remember what happens. It is precisely these spiritual choices that determine whether we live our lives with dignity.

Bread for the Journey, p.38:

Joy makes life worth living, but for many joy seems hard to find. They complain that their lives are sorrowful and depressing. What then brings the joy we so much desire? Are some people just lucky, while others have run out of luck? Strange as it may sound, we can choose joy. Two people can be part of the same event, but one may choose to live it quite differently from the other. One may choose to trust that what happened, painful as it may be, holds a promise. The other may choose despair and be destroyed by it. What makes us human is precisely this freedom of choice.

Dietrich Bonhoeffer, *Letters and Papers from Prison*, p.14:

It is infinitely easier to suffer in obedience to a human command than in the freedom of one's own responsibility. It is infinitely easier to suffer with others than alone . . . Christ suffered as a free man alone, apart and in ignominy, in body and spirit, and since then many Christians have suffered with him.

Letters and Papers from Prison, p.6:

Only now are the Germans beginning to discover the meaning of free responsibility. It depends on a God who demands responsible action in a bold ventured faith, and who promises forgiveness and consolation to a man who becomes a sinner in that venture.

Notes

Passages for meditation taken from:

Dietrich Bonhoeffer, *The Cost of Discipleship*, SCM, 2001
   Letters and Papers from Prison, SCM, 1971
   Life Together, SCM, 1954
Henri J. M. Nouwen, *Bread for the Journey*, DLT, 1996, and HarperSan-
Francisco, 1997
Used by permission.

Chapter 1: Freedom to Be Ourselves

1. From a letter of Bede Griffiths, 15 April 1990, quoted in Shirley du
   Boulay, *Beyond the Darkness*, Rider, 1998, p.250.
2. A quotation used by a missionary friend from India, Dr Dorothy Millar,
   two days before she died on 9 March 2001, and shared afterwards by
   her husband Peter.
3. *Fortune's Rocks*, Abacus, 1999, p.281.
4. Quotations from Eileen Egan, *Such a Vision of the Street: the authorised
   biography of Mother Teresa*, Sidgwick & Jackson, 1985.
5. From Janet Morley (ed.) *Bread of Tomorrow*, Christian Aid/SPCK,
   1992, p.19. She links the meditation with John 1:14 and Hebrews
   13:13–14.
6. Tom Wright, *Reflecting the Glory*, BRF, 1997, pp.23–4.

Chapter 2: Freedom to Receive from Others

1. Kenneth Cracknell, *Justice, Courtesy and Love: theologians and
   missionaries encountering world religions, 1846-1914*, Epworth, 1995.
2. See Michael Ford, *Wounded Prophet: a portrait of Henri J. M. Nouwen*,
   DLT, 1999, and Henri Nouwen, *Adam, God's Beloved*, DLT, 1997, p.87.
3. Found by Michael Ford in the Yale Divinity School Archives and quoted
   on page 36 of the above biography.
4. From the film *Angels over the Net*, (The Company, Spark Productions,
   1995), quoted by Michael Fisher, ibid., p.34.
5. Andrew Wingate, *Encounter in the Spirit*, WCC, 1988, 1991.

Chapter 4: Freeing Others to Be Themselves

1. A full article on Fuengsin and what I learned from her theologically and pastorally is available in *Theology*, May/June 1997, pp.170–9, entitled 'A Woman of Faith Dies: Death of a champion of Buddhism'.
2. From *I Care about your Happiness: quotations from the love letters of Kahlil Gibran and Mary Haskell*, Athena International, 1977, pp.28 and 29.
3. Max Olivia sj, *Free to Pray, Free to Love*, Ave Maria Press, Notre Dame, 1994, pp.33–5.
4. SCM, 1985.
5. For the material in this paragraph see the recent book by R. S. Sugirtharajah, *The Bible and the Third World*, Cambridge, 2002, Part 3, and Kinukawa, *Women and Jesus in Mark: a Japanese feminist perspective*, Maryknoll, Orbis Books, 1994.
6. *Good News in our Times: the Gospel and contemporary cultures*, Church House Publishing, 1991, Report of the Mission Theology Advisory Group, pp.24 and 25.
7. The full list, with accompanying commentary is found on pages 36–8 of *Good News in our Times*.

Chapter 5: Freedom and Conversion

1. Dag Hammarskjöld, *Markings*, Faber & Faber, 1964, p.169.
2. *Varieties of Religious Experience*, Longman, 1902.
3. *Encyclopaedia of Theology*, Burns & Oates, p.291.
4. *Understanding Conversion*, University Press of Virginia, 1992, and *Conversion and Text*, Virginia, 1992.
5. See my book, *The Church and Conversion*, ISPCK, Delhi, 1997, reprinted for SPCK, London, 1999.
6. *The Go-between God*, SCM, 1972, pp. 136–7 and 188–9.
7. *Markings*, op.cit., p.169.
8. Elie Wiesel, *And the Sea is Never Full*, London, HarperCollins, 2000, p.147.
9. As heard quoted in an ordination sermon in Leicester Cathedral, July 2001.

Chapter 6: Freedom to Choose

1. This was read at a funeral. Exact reference is unknown.
2. *Dying we Live: the final messages and records of some Germans who defied Hitler*, edited by Gollwitzer, Kuhn and Schneider, Harvill Press, 1956.
3. *Markings*, Faber, 1964, p.134.
4. Ibid., p.110.